The Language of Joy

by

Christopher Hamel Cooke

The Language of Joy

Ah heavenly joy! But who hath ever heard,
Who hath seen joy, or who shall ever find
Joy's language? There is neither speech nor word;
Nought but itself to teach it to mankind.

Robert Bridges (1844-1930)

by

Christopher Hamel Cooke

BOOK PUBLISHERS

© Christopher Hamel Cooke, 1994

World rights reserved by the publisher

Arthur James Limited
One Cranbourne Road
London N10 2BT
Great Britain

telephone: 0181 883 1831; fax: 0181 883 8307

British Library Cataloguing-in-Publication Data.
A catalogue record for the title is available
from the British Library

ISBN 85305 331 6

Cover design by
The Creative House, Saffron Walden, CB10 1EJ

Typeset by
Stumptype, London N20 OQG

Printed and bound by
Guernsey Press, Guernsey, Channel Islands

Cover Picture: *Le Sourire de Rheims*. The smiling angel is part
of the West Front of Rheims Cathedral

CONTENTS

FOREWORD
by the Rev Dr Denis Duncan
formerly Director of The Churches' Council
for Health and Healing
presently Managing Director of Arthur James Limited

I wrote in the Foreword to Christopher Hamel Cooke's most recent book, *A Time to Laugh*, that he "would not want an anthology of humorous tales, quips and stories to be his main memorial. It won't be for there is an exposition of a theology of joy to come, and that will be a profound book indeed".

That book has now arrived and it is indeed a profound book.

One of the great joys and privileges of having been closely associated with Christopher Hamel Cooke when he was Rector of St Marylebone in London was being brought into contact with other traditions than one's own, and more than that, being involved in them. Such ecumenical sharing can only be a blessing. I enjoyed reading and editing *The Language of Joy* in manuscript form because I felt I was learning all the time. It is that kind of book. It is full both of information about, and insight into, a field perhaps unfamiliar to many in any detail, namely the realm of the Mysteries — Joyful, Sorrowful and Glorious. For that reason alone, I commend this book to you.

Christopher Hamel Cooke is what we call in Scotland "a lad o' pairts". He has many gifts and talents. In his first book, *Health is for God*, his prophetic vision in conceiving the idea of a centre of healing and counselling working in co-operation with a National Health Service practice, a music therapy unit and various healing organisations, and his strength in carrying through such a £2 million project to completion are established for all time. His second book, *A Time to Laugh*, demonstrated his outstanding ability as a raconteur of humorous tales and many are the peals of laughter his book has caused. But behind the humourist, the visionary, the facilitator, the administrator is a man equipped theologically and trained pastorally who has much to offer in these fields. *The Language of Joy* is the book that illustrates his theological understanding and his capacity to explain profound concepts in words everyone can appreciate and understand.

It is a privilege and a pleasure for Arthur James to have been the publisher of three books by Christopher Hamel Cooke. *The Language of Joy*, honoured by a launch, following Choral Eucharist, in Coventry Cathedral will certainly be a book by which he will be happy to be remembered.

In presenting Arthur James' 1995 Lent Book, we express our gratitude to the Provost of Coventry Cathedral, the Very Rev John Petty, for his co-operation in making possible the launch and also for writing the Preface. We thank too the Bishop of Coventry, the Rt Rev Simon Barrington-Ward, for his commendation of the book.

We feel this book can well serve as the basis of a Lenten course this year, and in years to come, and hope it will be so used.

PREFACE
by John Petty

"The Kingdom of God is the sum of right relationships."
So wrote Archbishop William Temple in the first half of this
century.

And so writes Christopher Hamel Cooke in this last decade.
With similar insights, he says:
" 'Thy kingdom come', said so frequently in the Lord's
Prayer, means —

> To those set over us is due respect and obedience
> To the less fortunate is due compassion
> To the difficult is due understanding
> To our enemies is due both forgiveness and penitence
> To all is due gentleness."

Follow that and all relationships fall into place. Follow that
and his kingdom will come.

It is not easy to be respectful and obedient to the referee
"set over us" in a football match when we disagree with his
whistle and decisions, but the "forgiveness and penitence"
suggested means "Sorry, Ref" and suddenly the man in
authority smiles his acknowledgement and there is a glimpse
of joy.

Coventry Cathedral is not a football pitch but it has an open
air arena with two similar words displayed at one end "Father
Forgive". It has the Ruins of St Michael's Cathedral, bombed
in the Second World War; no roof but walls the colour of
jagged gums reminding us of human sin and then, engraved
on the sanctuary wall in gold, those two words, placed there
by Provost Dick Howard in 1940; not the full sentence of Our
Lord on the cross: "Father forgive them for they know not
what they do" but just the first two words, because as Dick
Howard said, we *all* need forgiveness.

It is the key to right relationships and the kingdom of God
and it still brings thousands every year to stand and ponder,
then step into the new Cathedral alongside; to walk from

Good Friday to Easter; to have a glimpse of joy.

Perhaps that is why Christopher Hamel Cooke turned to the present Provost to pen a preface. Christopher's long ministry brought him, for several years as Vicar, close to the Cathedral. We both share a total commitment to the ministry of prayer and healing in which we look for wholeness in body, mind and spirit. But there are differences. Christopher is a theologian. You will find the odd word in Greek (with its translation!). I come from a science stable so read this wonderful book from a different perspective. I *picture* a cross-section of the pyramid he describes in Chapter 2 and draw an elevation

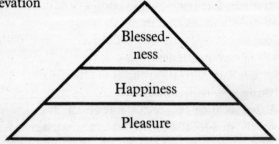

and then place alongside it his description:

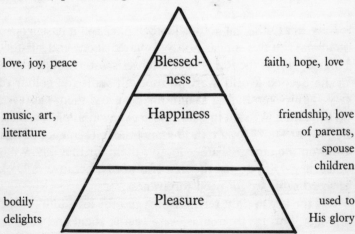

Then I can add on because . . .

'pleasure' for me conjures up the picture of an ITV 'ad' with Dad looking after his older child while Mum is in the maternity ward giving birth to number two. Dad, in desperation, is out to *please* his responsibility and serves up supper, the two favourite foods on the same plate — choc-ice and chips!

But this 'pleasure' moves on to 'happiness' when the story is shared with Mum and becomes 'history' in the family, to be recounted and laughed at in subsequent years, "Do you remember"? over the Sunday dinner table, when under Mum's guidance, the ice-cream comes after the potatoes on a separate plate!

And the 'blessedness' comes when the family turns from the past to the future and lets the children leave the 'nest', when the 'phone call or the scribbled postcard speaks of a bond that is all the stronger for letting go. 'Happiness' becomes 'joy' and page 35 comes alive for me.

And so the picture grows:

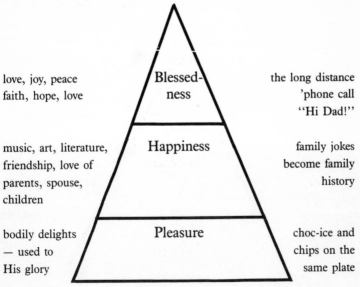

love, joy, peace
faith, hope, love

Blessed-
ness

the long distance
'phone call
"Hi Dad!"

music, art, literature,
friendship, love of
parents, spouse,
children

Happiness

family jokes
become family
history

bodily delights
— used to
His glory

Pleasure

choc-ice and
chips on the
same plate

Maybe *you* could write in *your* illustrations on the right hand side? Away from the family analogy, perhaps on the lines of peace, from the pleasure of fishing to the happiness of the musical tingle factor, to the joy of helping someone out of prison through Amnesty International.

What I have tried to suggest is that this book, written by a priest after many years of ministry, touches on the truths that affect us deeply but they are expressed in a way that can become real for us all. Christopher has the gift of the person that novelist, Susan Howatch, reveals in her Starbridge books. It is the spiritual director, a person of love, warmth, generosity, prayer and insight, underwritten by a sense of humour, who can laugh as I do at Charles Spurgeon's remark, quoted by Christopher: "When you speak of Heaven, your whole face should light up; when you speak of Hell — well, your usual face will do!" For me Christopher's most illuminating words came from his observation about the disciples at the Ascension:

They were filled with joy
and with the Holy Ghost.

(Acts 13.52)

It is almost impossible to read the verse without understanding it as saying that joy and the Holy Ghost are to all intents synonyms.

May you, the reader, be filled with joy and the Holy Spirit.

John Petty
Provost
Coventry Cathedral
Eve of Lent, 1995.

INTRODUCTION

This book is about Joy, the second of the fruits of the Spirit listed by St Paul in his Epistle to the Galatians (5.22). It is about laughter, the sacrament of Joy, its outward and visible (and audible) sign. It is about pleasing God and pleasing others — giving and making pleasure. It is about the healing power of joy and laughter, the recognition of the therapeutic value of making people joyful, making them laugh. It is also a reminder that the fruits of the Spirit are not primarily a means to another end, but ends in themselves. To have them is to be healthy. Not to have them is to be sick. In the first Epistle to the Corinthians, Paul lists "faith, hope and love" as the three great and abiding virtues. Faith and love then feature in both Epistles. Neither list is exhaustive, nor is it meant to be. All are marks of the 'whole man', fruit of the indwelling Spirit. They make us Christ-like, because they all find their fullest expression in the incarnate life of the Lord.

This is, then, also a book about healing — in the widest sense of that much-overworked word. It is concerned to say that the world is meant to be both a virtuous and a joyful place. Where it is not, it is sick and needs healing. The true Christian is, according to St Paul, to be in a permanent state of exultation. "Rejoice in the Lord alway: and again I say 'Rejoice'" (Phil. 4.4). Among his many admonitions to the Thessalonians he writes: "Rejoice evermore" (I Thess. 5.16). Christian joy is a state of blessedness, depending upon no outward circumstance. It comes from the Christ-centred life so that even suffering, for Christ's sake, ought to bring joy. Indeed the Thessalonians rejoiced precisely because they had suffered for their acceptance of Him. (I Thess. 1.6). Paul faces the prospect of martyrdom with joyfulness in which he asks his Philippian converts to share (Phil. 2.17-18). Nor should this surprise us since our Lord himself taught his disciples to rejoice and exult whenever men reproached, persecuted and slandered them (Matt. 5.11-12).

I have to confess that I find this injunction very difficult, and I have rarely found among my fellow Christians many who even try to obey it! The normal and usual reaction to persecution and slander is to attempt, by any means, to rebut the charges, which are so clearly to us unjustified and unjustifiable. Our feelings are hurt, our minds rebel against the injustice. We must clear our name. Our Lord's admonition, however, entirely invalidates this response. We are to rejoice and to be exceeding glad when we are so reproached. The motivation for the right response can come only from the remembrance of Christ's own prayer for his executioners: "Father, forgive". Christ's words in the Sermon on the Mount were put to a fearful test on that other mount, outside the city wall, and he was not found wanting.

Most of those who read these words will not be in the category of expectant martyrs. All of us though, have to witness to the Gospel and many of us find it painful to do so in some situations. The cross comes to most of us in the form of "sawdust and match-stick". We suffer petty irritation and hurt feelings. But the principle remains the same. We are meant to rejoice in the process and to find our healing as we do so.

We may need help. When people come for Christian Counselling their attitudes and presuppositions may, and probably will, need healing. They will need spiritual direction. It has long been my contention that the Church must provide, for those who seek its pastoral care, all three — counselling, healing and spiritual direction. Whichever they may ask for, they should be offered all three for these are an indivisible trinity. To say this is immediately to demonstrate the difference between the Christian approach and secular counselling. In the crypt at St. Marylebone in London we set up The Healing and Counselling Centre where this was the norm by which we worked. It was the particular contribution of the then Chaplain, the Reverend Valerie Makin, to combine in her own ministry, her gift of healing, her skill as a spiritual director and her pastoral counselling. For every church the emphasis would be different but the principle is the same.

"The Kingdom of God", says Paul in his letter to the Romans, "is not meat and drink, but righteousness and peace and joy in the Holy Ghost" (Romans 14.17). We are fortunate indeed when meat and drink accompany the spiritual qualities, and are in fact the outward expression of them. Our Lord turned water into wine at a wedding at Cana as a sign of the kingdom.

St John uses a different word for miracle from the other Evangelists. It is better translated as 'sign'. John wants us to see in these remarkable events signs of the advent of the kingdom. Using the Jewish water-pots as the receptacles of the new wine is seen by some as a parable of the overthrow of the Old Covenant which those water-pots represent. The manifestation of Christ's glory is the sign of his coming Kingdom and the occasion of the disciples' belief. We would not be pressing the story too far to suggest that as it is the presence of Christ which occasions the transformation of water into wine so his presence, then and still, transforms sorrow into joy. It cannot have been by accident that the first of the Lord's signs was performed at a wedding. The occasion and the event were surely chosen to demonstrate that meat and drink may be compatible with the advent of the kingdom, and indeed are meant to be.

Let us now turn our attention to a consideration of the Cardinal Virtues — Prudence, Temperance, Justice and Fortitude — seen in the light of the Theological Virtues, Faith Hope and Love. We shall see later that no joy can be called Christian if its object is not virtuous.

CHAPTER 1

THE JOY OF VIRTUE

"Joy is peace for doing what we ought to have done"
John Donne (d. 1631)

It is often protested, and rightly so, that Christianity is more than a moral code. Yes, but it is not less than one either. It demands of its adherents the striving after perfection (Matt. 5.48). When and where our innocence is lost, only penitence can make good that loss. Moral conduct is not however the prerogative of the Christian. It is taught by other faiths too. Christianity in its formularies depends upon Plato and Aristotle and their teaching concerning the good life. The so-called Cardinal Virtues, classified as prudence, temperance, fortitude and justice, were taken over by the chief Christian moral theologians, St Ambrose, St Augustine and St Thomas Aquinas and were contrasted with the Theological Virtues, Faith, Hope and Charity. No consideration of Christian joy can be adequate if it does not recognise the demands for right conduct. Joy and sin cannot co-habit! So as a preface to our study, we shall consider the Cardinal Virtues in the context of Joy, commenting on them in terms of Faith, Hope and Charity.

The Cardinal Virtues have been described as part of the "furniture of the human mind". Not themselves essentially Christian, faith alone can raise and direct them aright. They then become definitely Christian and can only reach perfection through faith and by God's grace. In combination, they become the backbone of the Christian character and the ground of true sanctity.

The perfection to which our Lord calls his followers is not capable of immediate attainment. It is the goal and end of all Christian endeavour. Nothing excuses us from the unwearying struggle to attain it. It is the common vocation of all human kind. Our prayer is that "our hearts may surely there be fixed — where true joys are to be found" (Collect for Easter iv, Book of Common Prayer).

(1) PRUDENCE

In his Epistle to the Ephesians (5.8) St Paul refers to the riches of God's grace "which he made to abound toward us, in all wisdom and prudence". What is prudence? It has been described as "a right judgment in practical matters". So prudence regulates our conduct and behaviour with regard to a specific and definite end. It is concerned with the best and the safest method of attaining that end and with whether it is, in fact, good and safe to pursue a particular end. It asks the question: if the end is not attained, what evil and what danger will follow?

Prudence guides the statesman and equally the thief! A good man will seek to be prudent and so will the evil man. But when we speak of Christian prudence, prudence in the context of faith, we immediately limit it to the end and purpose of the good life; the God-centred, Spirit-directed life. The selfish prudence of the man or woman's ambitions for their own success, seeking only their prudence is not Christian prudence. Worldly prudence has no ideals, runs no risks, sees the Cross as foolishness and always seeks to strike a balance between (the dimly perceived) morality of Christ and that of the world. Christian prudence reconciles man to God, seeks always the will of God as paramount and judges everything by this yard-stick.

Christian prudence is then super-natural. Faith and hope, our love for God and our fellow creatures, alone can sustain it. It then becomes the directing power of God's Holy Spirit. Possessed of it, the Christian ceases the endless weighing up of 'pros and cons'. He seeks to know God's will. He seeks the grace to pursue it.

How does he/she do these things?

Counsel is one of the gifts of the Spirit (Isaiah 11.2). It is mediated to and through our own experiences and our knowledge of that of others. It is mediated through our intercourse with those whose integrity and wisdom we value. Caution restrains the hasty decision, but from a decision to which we have properly come, there must be no looking back and no procrastination in implementing it, when we know, as surely as we can, that this is the way in which we must walk.

When the author of the Epistle to the Hebrews wrote his exhortation "to run with patience the race that is set before us" he continued: "looking unto Jesus the author and perfector of faith, who *for the joy that was set before him*, endured the cross, despising shame and hath sat down at the right hand of the throne of God".

It is one of the major paradoxes of the Christian life that although we pray that we may give and not count the cost, fight and not heed the wounds, labour and not seek any reward, yet the rewards are always offered and indeed promised.

The way of virtue laid out in the Beatitudes in the fifth chapter of St Matthew's gospel, promises reward for every virtue sought. "Blessed are the pure in heart, for they shall see God". Our Lord is deemed to have thought it prudent to walk in the way of the Cross "for the joy that was set before him". Prudence, like all virtues, may be 'infused' or 'acquired'. Theologians make the distinction between the virtues with which we are naturally endowed and those which we know we must acquire. All are, of course, God's gifts. The placid person does not need to struggle with a quick temper — he/she knows no such temptation. Their placidity is in the category of 'the infused'. Someone else may have to acquire such patience by the help of God's grace and to combat a relentless pressure to show anger. For some a high degree of prudence may be infused. For others we shall make excuse. "He means well" we say, or "He's temperamental".

Christians must not make such excuses for themselves. To rejoice and to give thanks for what God has already given them must be used to motivate the acquisition of what they do not yet have. This acquisition may be the by-product of a new control over sentiment or emotion or the eradication of avarice or ambition. Often we discover the futility of a direct approach to eradicate evil. It is the acquisition of virtue that achieves it. We do not seek to banish darkness, but to find the light.

(2) TEMPERANCE

It has been suggested that, although listed in second place, temperance is the most fundamental of the Cardinal Virtues. It is that upon which the other three depend.

In the New Testament, the Greek noun is translated in the Authorised Version by *soberness* or *sobriety*, as an adjunct to godliness. The equivalent adjective is rendered as *sober*, *temperate* or *discreet*. In its physical aspects, temperance is linked with self-control of the body, that being regarded as a "temple of the Holy Ghost". The early Fathers divided it into several other virtues, such as abstinence, chastity and modesty. In modern times there is a popular misconception that limits its application to the consumption of alcohol. This relates not so much to moderation as to total abstinence.

St Paul compares the Christian life to that of an athlete. In his first Epistle to the Corinthians he wrote: "Every man that striveth for the mastery is temperate in all things" (I Cor. 9.25). No virtue is more necessary to the athlete than temperance. Paul goes on, in succeeding verses, to say "I buffet my body and bring it into bondage". In the hierarchy of body, mind and spirit, he sees the body as subject to the mind, but it is not self-control with which Paul is concerned. It is *God's* control. The mind, under God's control, keeps the body in its right place.

Temperance has to do with the ordered use of all created

things. Man's sovereignty over nature has been grievously and grossly abused. The human predator has exploited and continues to exploit his custody of the planet. Temperance is not merely a personal and private virtue. Human kind needs to learn it and practise it. There are intemperate societies as well as intemperate people. The 'Green Movement' calls our attention to it. But at the individual level, temperance brings order to the Christian character as a God-given discipline. It is the enemy of and the corrective to the sin of gluttony. It enables us to recognise that God's gifts of food and drink, essential to our very existence, can be abused with damage done not only to our bodies but to our souls as well.

St Paul in writing to the Ephesians (4.26) says "Be ye angry and sin not". We can be, and often are, intemperate in our expression of anger. We lose rather than use our tempers. The much maligned virtue of meekness helps us to moderate how we give vent to our negative feelings, our disagreement with, and our disapproval of other people.

Temperance also adds to our freedom. We often use the word slavery of those who are addicted to alcohol or drugs. We might use it, too, of those who become obsessed with a particular hobby or sport. Their spare time is totally taken up with their preoccupation and they have no time to give away. Freedom from such slavery enables more important things to be done, more valuable ends to be sought. Temperance which for many people suggests a cold restraint or a puritanical negativism, is nothing of the sort. It brings a sense of liberation and a joy which depends upon the recognition of right priorities and their acceptance.

We must, of course, recognise that words in a living language change their meaning. Because this is so, the person who speaks or writes a particular word may mean something which the hearer or reader never grasps. The word temperance is a Latin word. It appears in the Revised Version for instance, in St Paul's Epistle to the Galatians (5.23) as part of the fruits of the Spirit and translates the Greek *egkrateia*, which could

23

be translated as self-restraint or continence. But when Paul wrote to the Philippians, he used the noun *to epieikes* which the RV translates as moderation, and has a suggestion of yieldingness and pliability. Moderation in modern English should have no suggestion of being moderate; for instance, moderately good or moderately self-restrained! The Greek word for the Cardinal Virtue, translated from Plato into Latin by Cicero is *sophrosune*. It is used in the Epistle to Titus (2.2) and translated there as temperate.

(3) JUSTICE

The word Justice does not appear in the New Testament, though it is frequently used in the Old, where it is a translation of the Hebrew *mishpat*. The New Testament equivalent is the Greek word *dikaiosune*. translated as 'righteousness'; the adjectival form is, of course, frequent and is translated as 'just'.

Justice can be defined as giving to all their due — to God due reverence, devotion, obedience and gratitude; to our fellow creatures, honesty, benevolence, forgiveness and compassion. To God and our fellow beings, the payment of what is due, is, or should be, both a duty and a joy.

Justice is the opposite of self-seeking and of all angry conflict with the interests of others. The source of justice and the grounds of its possibility lie in giving to God the love and adoration which are His due. Faith and hope and love are, for the Christian, essential pre-requisites of righteousness. We believe that to be God's will for us and for everyone. We hope unceasingly to see it established. Love alone sustains both faith and hope.

Justice is then the will to render to each and everyone their right. It is positive in promising what is right and due. It is negative in demanding that we abstain from any breach of right. So justice is often represented as holding scales, for its object is to arrive at an exact balance. If £100 is owed and

£99 paid, justice is not done. If £101 is paid, justice is exceeded by charity. My injustice damages anyone to whom I deny his or her due. But it damages me too. It is a blemish on the integrity of my character and robs me of the joy which the fulfilment of duty gives to those who perform it.

Every human being, unless born mentally defective, has the God-given capacity to know the meaning of right and wrong, and indeed has an innate love of right, as part of the "furniture of the soul". But we also believe, as Christians, that in Christ this is fully recognised as God-given, and as such is to be safeguarded and directed aright. So our Lord said: "Blessed are they that hunger and thirst after righteousness, for they shall be filled" (Matt. 5.6). Filled here means vindicated. Right will be seen to be right in the Kingdom of Christ and of God.

Christianity does not, of course, impose the duty of justice upon us. Rather does it help us to see that duty, and enable us, through God's grace, to fulfil it. So often people shy away from commitment to faith in Christ, fearing, as they say, an inability to fulfil its demands: "I could never live up to it". But faith does not add to our responsibilities. They are already there. Faith and her sisters, hope and love, enable them to be fulfilled. Righteousness and justice are not acts of grace except in so far as grace is required by all of us to honour our dues, both to God and to our fellow creatures.

The Athanasian Creed (*Book of Common Prayer*, "At Morning Prayer") reminds us that the Catholic Faith is to worship. That is its starting-point. We are to conduct our lives in such a way as to make our worship worthy; we do not worship to enable us to conduct our lives so. Worship is not a means to another end, though good things may follow from it. Worship is an end in itself. It is indeed *the* end and ultimate purpose of our existence. Once God is realised as God, worship is seen to be His right.

This concept of duty is vital to true religion and is the direccting force of mankind's life Godward. But love outstrips justice. Justice is not merely a duty but it is never less than a duty. Because we love God, we love to worship Him. We acknowledge that it is unjust not to pray, not to worship, for our failure to do so is to deny to God what is His due. But here, as in all else, the *theological* virtues outstrip the *cardinal* virtues. Justice towards God is inflamed by love, is informed by faith and is idealised by hope.

Let us now consider juistice in terms of our relationship to our fellow beings. "Our duty and our joy" sums up the disposition which should be that of every Christian as he or she seeks constantly to render to others what are their rights, what is their due.

There are, of course, not only people of other faiths, but people of no faith at all who put the rights of others before the pursuit of their own. But among Christians there should be no exception. "Thy Kingdom come" is the prayer which undergirds this and gives joy to the duty. To those set over us is due respect and obedience; to the less fortunate compassion; to the difficult, understanding; to our enemies both forgiveness and penitence; to all, gentleness.

As a matter of common experience, justice is denied by the bully in the school playground and by the legislator discriminsating against minorities in the community who are of a different faith or colour. The Christian, who by definition calls God his father, must in consequence call all people his brothers and sisters. If we are to love God, we are to love those whom God loves — all His creatures. Justice can only be done where faith reinforces the rule and charity provides the motive. "Thy Kingdom come" is both a petition and a statement of hope.

(4) FORTITUDE

We see at once how deeply interdependent are the Cardinal Virtues, as are the Theological. Faith, hope and love are an indivisible trinity. They are three aspects of one whole. So prudence, temperance and justice depend upon fortitude. They are none of them safe without it. Fortitude is the triumphant resistance to all that hinders the will of God. It is the spirit of enduring resistance and is concerned to see that the triumphs over the trials and temptations of life, are ultimate. Industry, thoroughness, moral courage, righteous indignation — these are all aspects of the virtue that can know no ending so long as this life, our life, continues. Fortitude is the spirit that ensures that this is so.

The word fortitude, is not, as such, a biblical term. The nearest equivalent to it is the Greek word *hupomeno*, usually translated as 'endure'. In St Matthew's Gospel (10.22) we read: "Ye shall be hated of all men for my name's sake, but he that endureth to the end, the same shall be saved". Paul, in his hymn to Love (I Cor. 13) says of love that it "hopeth all things, endureth all things". In II Tim. 2.10, the writer says: 'I endure all things for the elect's sake". The author of the Epistle to the Hebrews says of our Lord that he "endured the cross, despising the shame".

Endurance then is often linked with hardships. It is the quality that enables us to have the victory over them. Fortitude, with its root meaning of *fortis*, that is 'strong', suggests hostility. The Christian virtues are not popular. The Christian expects hindrance, opposition and ridicule. Non-Christians may expect them too. The difference is, first, the spirit in which the Christian meets the difficulties, and, secondly, the opposition which he or she encounters simply because they are Christians. There is, in both cases, strength more than their own.

Nowhere is this made more evident than by St Paul in his second letter to the Corinthians. He wrote (II Cor. 4.7):

We have this treasure (the spirit of illumination
and life) in earthen vessels, that the exceeding
greatness of the power may be of God and not from
ourselves; we are pressed on every side, yet not

27

straitened; perplexed yet not unto despair; pursued, yet not forsaken; smitten down, yet not destroyed; always bearing about in the body the dying of Jesus, that the life also of Jesus may be manifested in our body.

Of this passage, H L Goudge in his commentary on II Corinthians says this:

There is perhaps in St Paul's Epistle no passage deeper than this or more directly practical... How did the cross and, through the cross, the resurrection, come to the Lord himself? They came to him because in all his human weakness he set himself to carry out the task which the Father had given him... So it is with the work of the Church. Both the cross and the resurrection must come by facing the whole task — physical, intellectual and spiritual — and setting ourselves, just as we are, to accomplish it... The penalty of sin is not work, but over-work (Genesis 3.17-19) and so the cross comes. It is not God's intention that we should be in ourselves adequate to our task, but that we should be inadequate — not strong enough, or clever enough, or possessed of sufficient knowledge, to have humanly speaking, any chance of accomplishing it... The Church is always in a crisis, and always will be. Difficulties, limitations, insuperable problems, want of men and money, a menacing outlook, endless misunderstandings — we have not just to do our work in spite of these things; they are precisely the conditions required for the doing of it and the proofs that we are at grips with our real task.

Endurance, staying power, and learning to glory in our afflictions because they are the evidence that we are where God wants us to be — these are the qualities of Christian fortitude. The Psalmist wrote: "O that I had wings like a dove, for then would I fly away and be at rest". The temptation to apostasy has never been more vividly portrayed. To resist such temptation requires of us, fortitude.

Apostasy is expressed in one word, in I Samuel 4.21. The word is *ichabod*. It was the name given by Eli's daughter-in-law to her new-born son as she herself lay dying. "The Glory is departed from Israel" she said, "for the ark of God is taken". Fortitude in the hour of death and defeat was not for her. Many a Christian has been tempted to cry 'Ichabod' in the face of overwhelming disaster. But the cross points to an altogether different response, however hard it may be to make it. Fortitude is opposed to fear. It is opposed, too, to recklessness. It demands of us a magnaminity — a greatness of soul — which faith alone can provide. It requires of us munificence, a generosity beyond mere human giving. It involves the patient endurance of which Christ is our great example — and our only enabler.

So the Cardinal Virtues prudence, temperance, justice and fortitude, can rightly be described as the "backbone of the Christian character" when they are considered in the light thrown on them of the Theological Virtues, of faith, hope and love.

This is a book about joy, but there is no joy to equal that of duty well done — that is to God's Glory, in the service of our fellow creatures and as a blessing to ourselves. Our further considerations are to give flesh and blood to the backbone and skeleton.

CHAPTER 2

PLACEBO

Placebo means "I shall please". The Latin verb has become an English noun. Simply understood the word is applied to a doctor's prescription which has no medicinal value whatever. Because it pleases the patient, and he or she imagines that it has curative effects, it in fact proves beneficial. Where the source of sickness is in the heart or mind of the patient and the physical symptoms are the expression of such malaise, a placebo will often work wonders.

A pejorative quality should not be attached to the word. The phrase "only a placebo" does not do justice to its real worth. To please the patient is important, perhaps all important. By whatever honest means that is achieved is great gain. The doctor's bed-side manner, the social worker's unfeigned acceptance of the client, the priest's non-judgemental attitude — all these things please patients, make them *feel* better and in fact enable them to *be* better.

It is in the psychosomatic field that the placebo principle is important — and all sickness has a psychosomatic dimension. To be chronically displeased is to be sick and will often evince physical symptoms. Temporary displeasure is often described in physical terms. "So-and-so is a real pain in the neck", we say. We may refer to other parts of the anatomy, if we wish to emphasise the point.

Many years ago in the context of a particular hospital ward, where I was Chaplain, I used to carry out a ward round immediately after the Consultant Physician had completed his. He had a reputation for being a first class doctor and a brilliant diagnostician. But his round upset the ward on a regular weekly basis, because he bullied his patients. He thoroughly displeased them, in the short term, however efficacious was his medicine in the long term. His bed-side manner had an immediate deleterious effect.

31

All of us, in all our dealings with one another, except in the most superificial of relationships, are either pleasing or displeasing our neighbours. Our words are a blessing or a curse — to a greater or lesser extent. Our silence may be healing or damaging. It is not only in a professional relationship that this is true but in all the contacts all of us make. Giving pleasure, imparting joy, making people smile or laugh, these things are all of God. To please Him is the whole duty of man.

There is a proper sense in which the idea of pleasing or displeasing God seems presumptuous in the extreme. How can the behaviour of one among millions possibly make any difference to God? Our part is so infinitesimal that it must surely be irrelevant. To attribute pleasure or displeasure — changing moods — is also contrary to traditional teaching about God, which is summed up, for instance, in the Church of England's 39 Articles. They begin with the assertion that God is "without body, parts or passions". Yet it surely lies at the heart of Judaeo/Christian doctrine that our thoughts, words and works are known to God, are pleasing or displeasing to Him and do effect our relationship with Him. Holistic theology bears witness to the fact that no one is truly whole who is not in a right relationship with God. Holiness is not only part of health but its ultimate expression. In the Old Testament God's displeasure was often supposed to produce instant judgement. While the Book of Job is a profound attempt to disprove the immediate connection between sin and suffering, it never suggests, however, that sin does not displease God or righteousness have the opposite effect.

In the first book of the Kings (I Kings 3), the Lord appears to Solomon in a dream and says, "Ask what I shall give thee". Solomon asks for "an understanding heart... that I may discern between good and bad". We then read (v.10): "The speech pleased the Lord that Solomon had asked this thing". This episode not only makes it clear that God could indeed be pleased (or otherwise) but also that God's gifts depend not only upon His bounty but also upon our wish to receive them. There is a real sense in which Solomon asked for what he already had. The wisdom which he chose showed wisdom. It also showed humility, without which wisdom cannot be truly wise.

If this story shows God well pleased, let us turn to another story, concerning his father, David. It is the sordid account of his seduction of his neighbour's wife, Bathsheba. Her husband, Uriah, is fighting the Philistines when the seduction takes place. When David discovers she is pregnant, he sends a message to the battle front that Uriah is to be placed ''in the forefront of the hottest battle'' where he is inevitably killed. David then marries Bathsheba. But the chapter ends with the very simple but vital statement: ''The thing that David had done displeased the Lord''.

There is one further point about these stories that needs to be made. In my experience, the Bible is often referred to for moral guidance with the implicit suggestion that a thing is bad if the Bible forbids it, and good if the Bible enjoins it. Surely the truth of the matter is that the Bible condemns some things because they are evil — not the other way round. It commends certain things because they are good — not the other way round. Adultery and murder are not wrong because they displease the Lord. They displease the Lord because they are wrong.

When we turn to the New Testament, we again find the criteria of pleasing and displeasing the Lord. In St John's Gospel for instance (8.29), our Lord says: ''He that sent me is with me: The Father hath not left me alone; for I do always that thing that pleaseth Him.'' The implication here is that to displease God is an act of separation from Him, a deliberate choice on our part. To please God is to find Him with us.

The context is very different but the lesson the same in St Mark's Gospel (10.14) when the disciples rebuked those who brought children to him for his touch. We read that ''when Jesus saw it, he was much displeased''. His pleasure was in

33

their presence with him and he was displeased with those who kept them apart from him.

In Romans 8, verse 8, St Paul says "They that are in the flesh cannot please God". An earlier verse suggests that 'in the flesh' means to be 'carnally minded'. How does this concept relate to a holistic approach to healing, where the *body* is always linked with the *mind* and the *spirit* as a trinity in unity? St Paul often seems to suggest that the *body* is to be regarded as an enemy and the source of human depravity. We know, of course, that the greatest evils in the world have not been occasioned by those who have over-rated or over-worked the sensual and physical side of their natures. The evils perpetrated by, for example, Stalin or Hitler, came from the depravity of their minds, not their bodies. But to be 'carnally minded' means to be so exclusively concerned with the body and its appetites, that the mind and the spirit are wholly subordinated to the pursuit of fleshly pleasures. In that sense those 'in the flesh' cannot please God. But does it follow that to give the flesh a place, an appropriate place, is displeasing to God? Certainly not, for the body is His handiwork as surely as the mind and the spirit. I have sometimes suggested that the good things of this life can be thought of as pleasure, happiness and blessedness. Let me enlarge:

In pyramid form the bottom level of life's good things consists of the bodily delights, God-given and to be used and enjoyed as His gifts and to His glory. They are transient. Robert Burns wrote:

Pleasures are like poppies spread
You seize the flower the bloom is shed
Or like a snow fall in the river
A moment white, then melts for ever.

To be mindful *only* of life's pleasure would be a sorry condition indeed.

Happiness is something more. It consists in the appreciation of music and art, the enjoyment of literature, the cultivation of friendship, the love of parents, spouse and children. More lasting than pleasure, it is still however transient.

The scale of blessedness is the realm of the things of the spirit:- love, joy, peace; faith, hope and love. These are the things of which heaven is made. We have them here; we shall take them with us there.

When St Paul speaks of the 'natural body' and the 'spiritual body' he implies that in the life of the world to come the body which will then be ours will be different from the one adapted to our natural state here on earth. As we grow spiritually we are, as it were, nurturing that spiritual body. If on earth we are body, mind and spirit, so shall we be in eternity. The transformation from natural to spiritual may be beyond our comprehension but the process is the purpose of life's journey. As God is both the goal of our journey as well as our companion on it, so our spiritual body is being fashioned now as well as being that with which we shall be endowed at journey's end.

Pleasure, happiness, blessedness — all are God-given. The last is not only the greatest and most important of the three. It over-arches the other two. We can separate them in order to analyse and discuss them but in truth they are inseparable. Pleasure can, of course, occur in an un-Godly or even a sinful context. We can take pleasure of a sort in evil things. But this only reminds us of 'the Fall', of 'Original Sin', of the fact that the world and everything in it are not as they should be. Pleasure can be tainted but always it is thereby diminished not enhanced. Pleasure can be and should be blessed by God and when it is, it partakes of that blessedness of which heaven is made. Happiness likewise is greatly enhanced when it seeks God's blessing and its source is ascribed to Him.

We have long been learning the error of trying to separate body, mind and spirit as if they were each parts of a whole. We now know more clearly than we used to, that they are rather differing modes of our being, each dependent upon the other and none having a life of its own. So pleasure, perhaps most easily associated with the body, happiness, most easily associated with the mind and blessedness, with our spiritual nature — these three are also one and indivisible. All are God's gifts. All are to be used to His glory. Faith is that which enables them to be so. Without faith, it is impossible to please Him (Heb. 11.6).

A constant theme of Christian apologetics is the relationship between the Passion of Christ and the sin of man. Our sins we recognise as the cause of his Passion and his Passion as the expiation of our sin. We have already said that the obverse of this supreme truth is enlarged upon too little. If my sin hurts the heart of God, my penitence must be pleasing to Him. Did not our Lord himself say:

> Joy shall be in Heaven over one sinner that repenteth (Luke 15.7)?

It is humbling indeed to realise that just as our wrong actions 'add' to the Passion of the Lord, so our penitence actually contributes to the joy of Heaven itself.

Let us see how laughter features in the Scriptures, since laughter is the expression of joy.

CHAPTER 3

LAUGHTER IN THE SCRIPTURES

We have seen how extensive are the references to joy and to giving pleasure in the Scriptures. But what place is given to laughter?

Most of the references make the verb 'to laugh' synonymous with 'to scorn'. In Psalm 2.4 we read:-

He that sitteth in the heavens shall laugh.

The Lord shall have them in derision.

God's own laughter is not then the expression of His joy but of His contempt for His enemies. We need not hesitate to say that the Psalmist ascribes to God his own feelings. Is the laughter of scorn an appropriate reaction in any circumstance, or is it evidence of man's depravity, a consequence of 'the Fall'? Certainly it is difficult to find any therapeutic value in such a reaction. To mock and to deride are not attributes of healing; they are not ingredients in pastoral care. Do they serve a prophetic purpose? To establish a right attitude, an orthodox point of view, does it help to deride those who see things differently? Surely not.

There can be no such cleavage between pastoralia and prophecy. What is inappropriate in one must be inadvisable in the other. Scorn is diabolic. It is destructive both for the subject and the objective of it. The laughter that accompanies and expresses it is not of God.

But the Scriptures do have some references to laughter and humour, both explicit and implicit. In Genesis 17 and 18 we read of Abraham's and Sarah's laughter at the announcement of her impending pregnancy. Both are elderly if not positively old. Sarah is afraid at having laughed and tries to conceal and to deny that she has done so. But that laughter must have been the immediate and joyful response to the Angel's message, made all the more joyful by its seeming impossibility. The laughter of incredulity in such situations is not an offence

39

to the bearer of such tidings, but on the contrary would normally add to their pleasure as the bearer of good, though highly improbable, news.

Laughter as an expression of joy is found elsewhere in the Old Testament. Psalm 126 opens with the words:

> When the Lord turned again the captivity of Zion
> we were like them that dream
> Then was our mouth filled with laughter
> And our tongue with singing.

So total is the joy, against the background of such sorrow, that again the reality seems incredible — like a dream. Laughter alone can express the delight.

In the New Testament when our Lord raised Jairus's daughter, we are told that when he said the maid was not dead but asleep, the by-standers "laughed him to scorn". Their incredulity was understandable, the mode of its expression inadmissable. They were made "to laugh on the other side of their faces". There is no record of apology, no admission of lack of faith, but "the fame thereof went abroad into all that land".

There is no other New Testament reference to laughter except in the general Epistle of St James (4.9) where he exhorts his readers, "Be afflicted and mourn and weep. Let your laughter be turned to mourning and your joy to heaviness." James is concerned at the light-heartedness of his readers and exhorts them to penitence and a more serious mind. The laughter of levity, facetiousness in the face of the serious, the flippancy that is demonstrative of shallowness — in all such situations laughter is indeed unseemly and far from the expression of true Christian joy.

But the New Testament still has its amusing moments when laughter must have been evinced. In Matthew 15 (based on Mark 7) we read of our Lord's encounter with the woman of Canaan when he made his sortie into the coasts of Tyre and Sidon. Is it possible to read this story and not to recognise the playful nature of our Lord's dealings with the woman?

First, he does not answer. Then the disciples ask him to send her away. Next he proclaims that his ministry is exclusive to Israelites. Today he would have been accused of racism but the impression given is that he is making a statement ridiculing racism! Then he addresses the woman directly: "It is not meet to take the children's bread, and to cast it to dogs".

He uses a word which would be better translated 'little dogs' or even 'puppies'. She responds to this playful repartee: "Truth Lord, yet the dogs eat of the crumbs which fall from their masters' table".

The conversation ends with the granting of her request — her daughter's deliverance. But the conversation must have been one of healing for her for the Lord's way of handling her was a placebo indeed. A changed woman went home to a healed daughter. There must indeed have been laughter.

Translation sometimes obscures humour. An Italian proverb says: "The translator is a traitor". In St Matthew 16.18 we read: "I say unto thee, that thou art Peter and upon this rock I will build my church".

In so many languages the name Peter and the word Rock are the same. In English the pun is lost. Must there not have been smiles on the faces of all around when our Lord first said it? It would be especially so as rock-like characteristics were not Peter's strong points. These were virtues he would have to acquire rather than those with which he was naturally infused.

Fr Harry Williams in his book *Tensions* (Fount 1989) refers to the Resurrection of our Lord as "the supreme, the final, the ultimate joke" — that than which nothing could be funnier. He describes it so:

> Here are Caiphas and all his crowd ... they have
> done their duty ... efficiently disposing of a
> dangerous fool. He is safely dead ... But behind
> their backs the fool has popped up again and is
> dancing about even more vigorously than before and
> even more compellingly. People here, there and
> everywhere are falling under his spell.

CHAPTER 4

JOY IN THE SCRIPTURES

The Puritan through life's sweet garden goes
To pluck the thorn and throw away the rose
And seeks to please by this peculiar whim
The God who fashioned it and gave it him.

There is, of course, a place in Christian living for ascetisism. Hedonism needs its corrective. When drunkenness became a national vice, (and perhaps it is so still, or again), Methodism required of its membership teetotalism. It was a right and proper response and it made a difference.

There is Hedonism in most if not all of us. We need the Lenten fast, for instance, to do its corrective work. To abstain from laughter for a while may be good for the soul. To abstain from perfectly legitimate pleasures in order to fix the mind on higher things — who would contest the value of so doing? There is paradoxically joy to be found in the process. No one suggests the true ascetic is without joy in his or her life. Nevertheless the pleasures of this life are God-given and may properly be enjoyed. To condemn them is an overt criticism of God Himself.

Christianity is a joyful religion. Joy is one of the fruits of the Spirit. *Jubilate* is the cry of the church to its members. It was so in Judaism. It is so even more in Christianity. The evidence for this is that there are some one hundred references to joy in the Old Testament and about the same number in the New Testament which is less than one-third as long. With so many options to choose from any system of selection will be arbitrary. But a selection of examples will help to demonstrate the essentially joyful character of the Scriptures and dispel any suggestion that a long face and miserable spirit are conducive to the religion of either Testament.

Let us, in the Old Testament, look at the joy which was

meant to and usually did accompany some of the events of greatest significance:

The Creation (Gen. 1)

The Exodus (Ex. 15)

The Dedication of the Temple (I Kings 8.66)

The Discovery of the Law (Nehemiah 8).

The Scriptures begin with the story of Creation. In six days God made the world and all that it contains. He views what He has done and rests in contentment on the Sabbath. Joy is implicit rather than explicit but the story leaves one with no greater impression than God's pleasure in what He had done. The note of joy is unmistakably sounded.

Of course we know that chapter 2 of Genesis gives an alternative account of creation but what is really important is the recognition that the creation of the universe is not a long passed event described in two different ways even in Scripture, but a present and ongoing reality. God is *making* the world and we are held in being by His creative love. If joy accompanies creation, God rejoices now in what He is doing, rejoices in each new born babe, in each and every stage of our journey, in His animals and birds and insects, in His mountains and hills, rivers and valleys. *Benedicite omnia opera*, "O all ye works of the Lord, bless ye the Lord." As we learn to rejoice in God's saving work, so also must we learn to rejoice in His creative activity and to see ourselves as the mouthpieces of all that He has made and is making. Humanity sings "Benedicite" on behalf of all creation.

No event is of greater significance for the Jew than is the Exodus — for the Christian too, who sees it as a model of Christ's delivering his people from the bondage of sin. The response of the children of Israel to the deliverance from slavery in Egypt is found in Exodus 15.1-22. It is a Song of Joy to the Lord for what He has done: "Then sang Moses and the children of Israel this song unto the Lord and spake saying, 'I will sing unto the Lord for He hath triumphed gloriously'". As the Hebrews first used these words to celebrate the Exodus, so Christians use them still, of Christ's victory over sin and death.

I owe to Rabbi Curt Cassell an important observation here, typically Hebrew because told in story form.

The Israelites are rejoicing at their deliverance and the Angels, seeing and hearing them, join in. The Almighty reprimands them. They protest: "How can we not join in the celebration of your people?" they ask. But the Lord reminds them, "The Egyptians are also my people".

The giving of the Law however stands out as an example of apostasy, and rejoicing of entirely the wrong sort. Moses was given two tablets of stone "written with the finger of God" but when he returned from Mount Sinai, after a delay not to the liking of the Israelites, he found that Aaron his brother had made a calf for them to worship from their offerings of gold. Moses heard their rejoicing from afar — "the noise of them that sing do I hear" (Ex. 32.18). It is important to recognise that man is capable of the perversion of all God's gifts. Joy is no virtue unless its object is virtuous, as we have already seen. Let us see how a later generation made atonement for the apostasy of their forbears.

If we turn to the Book of Nehemiah we read how Ezra the scribe brought the Law before the congregation, and read aloud from morning until midday. The audience was deeply moved by the experience and Nehemiah's simple comment is: "The joy of the Lord is your strength" (Nehemiah 8.10). It may be difficult for twentieth century Christians to imagine the scene as Nehemiah describes it but I take his comment to mean that where people rejoice in the revealed will of God for them they will also find strength to obey it. John Seeley once wrote (it is quoted by N P Williams in his *Ideas of the Fall and Original Sin*):

No heart is pure that is not passionate
No virtue is safe which is not enthusiastic.

The Alternative Service Book of the Church of England has the delightful phrase: "It is our duty and our joy" to begin the Eucharistic prayer. The combination of duty and joy make for formidable motivation. Those whose lives generally find that joy and duty coincide are having the Book of Common Prayer Collect for Easter IV answered for them.

Grant unto thy people that they may love the thing which thou commandest and desire that which thou dost promise; that so among the sundry and manifold changes of the world, our hearts may surely there be fixed where true joys are to be found."

Peter Abelard in his hymn "O quanta qualia" (English Hymnal 465) describes heaven as the place where

Wish and fulfilment shall severed be n'er

Nor the thing prayed for fall short of the prayer.

The coincidence of duty and joy, of God's will and our pleasure, is heaven on earth.

E W Hunt in his *Portrait of Paul* wrote "Joy is an emotion the popular mind rarely associates with Christianity. The vulgar picture of the disciple of Christ shows one who resembles Don Quixote's El cabillero de la triste figura". How different is the portrait of the Christian painted by Paul! Like peace, joy is one of the signs of God's rule (Rom. 14.17). Christian joy is the lasting joy that comes from the Christ-centred life, the life of self-abnegation. So in turning to the New Testament we find that though there may be few references to laughter and little explicit humour, there is a great deal of joy! Indeed, the title "Joyful Mysteries" is often used of five early events, before and immediately after our Lord's birth.

(a) The Joyful Mysteries

Mystery has here no suggestion of the 'mysterious'. It is designed to point to the profundity of the occasions and to remind us that we can never fully comprehend or exhaust the meaning of them. We therefore begin our consideration of joy in the New Testament with the Annunciation to our Lady that she is to be the mother of our Lord (Luke 1.26-38).

The story of the Annunciation is designed to highlight the difference between the pregnancy of Mary and that of all other women. It is a 'virginal conception' that is described by St Luke (Luke 1.27). Incredulity is still the response of many, even among Christians. But the unique character of the conception of our Lord depends far more upon the subseqent events of his incarnate life than it does upon a unique conception. Has the story of the Angel Gabriel and the announcement made to Mary been written back into the Gospel to focus our attention, from the start, upon the unique character of the life of Christ? Or does it in itself account for that unique life? I have to admit that if the virginal conception could be disproved it would make no difference to my discipleship, nor to that, I suspect, of the vast majority of Christians. The Annunciation remains indeed a mystery, however our Lady perceived the event and became aware of her pregnancy, and however we enter into the joy that was hers. Nor must we ever fail to remember that every pregnancy is unique, every baby a special creation, to be wondered at and, in the sense that we have described elsewhere, to be worshipped.

It is not my intention here to argue the case for and against the termination of a pregnancy. Can it sometimes be the lesser of two evils? Perhaps — but it remains always an evil. Our Lady's perception of her pregnancy could ultimately be experienced only in ordinary human terms. She was unmarried. Could she possibly count on Joseph's understanding? She was very poor. Would not an abortion have been socially the best answer for her? Many women and girls claim that this is so with far less justification. Perhaps by putting such cases into this context we may perceive the evil of it more readily. Where pregnancy is robbed of its joy, it becomes sorrow indeed. Where does responsibility lie for so sad an eventuality? And where does grace come in and by whom is it mediated?

The birth narratives of St Matthew and St Luke both show that the event which divides time in two was not demanding of fear and dread. Of the Wise Men, Matthew wrote,

When they saw the star,

they rejoiced with exceeding great joy.

and St. Luke records the Angel saying to the Shepherds:

Fear not, for behold I bring you good tidings

of great joy, which shall be to all people.

We have seen in the Introduction that St John marks the beginning of the Lord's ministry at a wedding (John 2.1-11) while St Mark records the pleasure of the father at the advent of the son (Mark 1.11).

There came a voice from heaven, saying

"Thou art my beloved son in whom I am well pleased."

The second of the Joyful Mysteries is the Visitation of our Lady to her cousin Elizabeth, pregnant with John who was for ever after to be known as "The Baptist". That their meeting should be both natural and joyful is hardly surprising.

Both conceptions had been surrounded by remarkable, miraculous circumstances. Let us not forget that the word 'miracle' does not in itself carry with it the suggestion of divine intervention. It simply describes the reaction of the beholder. 'Miracle' comes from the Latin *admiro*, "I wonder at". Anything which causes the viewer to lift up his heart to God in wonder, love and praise is, by defintion, a miracle. Both Mary and Elizabeth had wondered at their conceiving — Mary because "she knew not a man", Elizabeth because she was past childbearing age. But both were pregnant. When Mary visited Elizabeth, the "babe leapt in her womb for joy" (Luke 1.44). Is there in human history any other instance of joy being ascribed to an unborn child? Sorrows enough awaited the two yet-to-be-born babies but at this pre-natal stage the 'quickening' which Elizabeth experienced at her cousin's arrival seemed to her to be an expression of joy.

The Visitation in one sense adds little to our understanding of the Incarnation, yet the story gives and teaches us so much. Elizabeth's joy is mixed with awe "that the mother of my Lord should come to me" (Luke 1.43). Mary goes on to speak the words ever since known as The Magnificat. Its words, based on I Sam. 2.1 where Hannah praises God for the birth of Samuel her son, have enriched Christian spirituality and piety throughout Christian history, and continue to do so. Mary's words of praise have been uttered in worship countless thousands of times and will be until time shall be no more.

The Visitation must also be able to tell us something about the nature of human encounter. Life it has been said is 'meeting' (not meetings!). We are only ourselves in relationship — to God, to others and to the things around us. In some monastic houses I am told that every ring of the bell or 'phone is treated as if our Lord were calling. In a sense he is. We encounter another image of God, and we ourselves are no less. The image is often so fearfully distorted that it becomes hardly recognisable.

Cuthbert Bardsley used to tell the apocryphal story of our Lord walking with his disciples and stumbling on the body of a dead dog. There were several expressions of horror and disgust but our Lord observed upon the beauty of its teeth. It is rare that some good cannot be found in the worst of humans, just as surely as some criticism *can* be made of the best of people. 'Total corruption' does not mean that anyone or anything is totally corrupt. It means rather that there is a degree of corruption in the totality of creation. One of the consequences of this truth is our propensity for singling out the evil and ignoring the good, for being far more eloquent with our criticism than our praise. By grace alone can this tendency be reversed. By grace alone do we learn to seek the source of joy in other people and to ignore or at least to minimize the importance of their faults and failings. "Charity

49

covers a multitude of sins". By this is meant, not that if we are generally charitable we can get away with a lot of shortcomings. Rather does it mean that *my* charity is meant to cover *the other person's sins* — cover, ignore, cease to notice, because we are too busy being generous about "the beauty of the teeth". Confrontation has become a pejorative word, but when the Christ in me meets the Christ in you, love, joy and peace ensue and abound.

Although of course unfortunate and sometimes sinful circumstance may prevent it being so, the knowledge that a baby is expected must, even at the natural level, be one of the most joyful realisations known to human experience. Perhaps there is always, for every future mother, a moment of being 'troubled', but this will again normally and naturally give place to the 'fiat', "be it unto me".

The third of the Joyful Mysteries is then the Nativity itself. We are all aware of the humble if not humiliating circumstances of our Lord's birth. We do well to remember that the virginal conception was originally seen as part of that humiliation rather than as a pointer to her 'purity'. Down the ages of Christianity there have been attempts to sanitize the manger and the stable, of which the clearest evidence is in the traditional paintings and the modern Christmas card. They convey little of the actuality with all its attendant unpleasantness. To do this is to detract from the Incarnation not to enhance it. Hymns and carols often tend to do the same thing. Consider; for example

The cattle are lowing
The baby awakes
The little Lord Jesus
No crying he makes.

Tears, to the author of these lines, would have been incompatible with the divinity of Christ, in the interest of which, part of his humanity has to be denied. Who was it who described a baby as being "a loud noise at one end and

50

total irresponsibility at the other''? If the Word was made flesh, that statement describes our Lord, like every other baby, more aptly than the words of ''Away in a manger''. Let not our joy in the birth of Christ depend upon its being made quite unreal.

But there is much more at stake than we may at first realise. The age-old problem is the reconciliation of the two natures of Christ, the divine and the human. To emphasise one at the expense of the other is to distort the Gospel. Sometimes the temptation is in one direction, sometimes in the other. The Nativity and its circumstances make for opportunity to lay to heart the true humanity of our Lord, just as the Annunciation points us in the other direction. A miraculous conception for the divine son of God is followed by a human birth just like every other human birth, only more so; more so because accentuated by the humble circumstances which surround it.

If every conception is in some sense miraculous, so is every birth. To emphasise the divinity of Christ we neither have to deny his humanity nor our own divinity. Each of us is a unique representation of God; all of us are made in His image and likeness. A new-born babe, indeed every new-born babe, is a new and unique image of the Creator, of God, the Father of us all. Babies are often idolised, and it is good that it should be so. But the real joy of every nativity surely depends upon the recognition of the great truth — a new likeness of God has come into the world, a new journey from earth to heaven has begun.

We read sometimes of babies who are neglected. That many die of starvation or in consequence of war cannot be denied. But some are deliberately neglected and suffer grievously in consequence. When we hear of such things we are properly outraged. Similarly a child who is denied proper schooling and education calls forth our indignation. Yet the spiritual neglect of children calls forth no such reaction. Babies may even be brought to baptism with no intention on the part of parents and godparents to bring them up in the faith. If only we could show that it is the joy of discipleship that is being withheld. Have we so emphasised duty, if we have emphasised anything at all, that joy has been forgotten? Have we so lost our own capacity for joy in the Lord that we cannot impart it to others? Birth is one of the most joyful experiences, for which mothers have traditionally minimized the pain which precedes it. The birth of our Lord is deemed by Christians to be the greatest event since Creation itself, dividing time into two, BC and AD. It is in the context of this event that we are to put every human birth. In the rite of Baptism it is customary to anoint the baby, and to name her or him. Covertly, if not overtly, we name the baby 'John Christ', 'Mary Christ'. The Nativity of our Lord was to make this true or to make this truth evident; at the font we proclaim it to be so.

The fourth of the Joyful Mysteries is the Presentation of Christ in the Temple.

"A time to weep" (Eccl. 3.4) would be an easy title to illustrate from the Scripture. No one would deny this, nor does this little book intend to suggest otherwise. There is sorrow in both Testaments, sorrow and tears in abundance. But there is joy too and joy is seen as a wholly appropriate response to the great events which the New Testament, as well as the Old, record. It is also true that our Lord teaches that we are to rejoice even in adversity. The Sermon on the Mount, beginning as it does with the Beatitudes (Matt. 5.1-12) requires of the readers, as I have observed in my Introduction, that they rejoice "when men shall revile you and persecute you, and shall say all manner of evil against you, falsely for my sake". Christ is the catalyst who turns sorrow into joy and tears into laughter. He said of his Kingdom (Matt. 13.44) that it is "like a treasure hid in a field, the which when a man hath found he hideth and for joy thereof goeth and selleth all that he hath, and buyeth that field."

Irony is frequent in the Gospels! The Presentation was the

occasion of Mary's 'Purification'. The immaculate mother of God submits, with the humility which was one of the hall-marks of her character, to the Jewish Law. Forty days after the birth of her son she goes to the Temple for the rite of Purification and to 'present' her first-born son. The women of Israel were considered to have contracted a legal stain in childbirth and were obliged to offer a young pigeon as a sin offering. Having done so they were then free to attend once more the ceremonies of divine worship. The offering of a second pigeon related to the fact that Jesus was a first-born son and thus consecrated to God from his birth. The irony of the second offering is as great as of the first! How could he who absolutely belonged to God, was indeed His unique son, be redeemed and freed from that position? Yet the second pigeon was offered. Such was the humility of the mother of God.

The church commemorates the Presentation on the fortieth and last day of Christmas, February 2nd, commonly known as Candlemas. This familiar name stems from the words uttered in the Temple by Simeon. Indeed the Festival was at one time known as 'The Meeting' (of Our Lord with Simeon and Anna).

To Simeon and to St Luke who records it, we owe the words:
   Lord, now lettest thou thy servant depart in peace
      According to thy word.
   For mine eyes have seen
      Thy salvation
   Which thou hast prepared
      Before the face of all people
   To be a light to lighten the Gentiles
      And to be the glory of thy people Israel.
                                        (Luke 2.29-32)
It is worth noticing the significance of some of the events of that day of meeting as well as the way in which a major part of Christendom has traditionally celebrated what is probably the most ancient of all the Festivals of our Lady.

Alcuin, in a homily written in AD 700, wrote: "The whole multitude of the city collecting together devoutly celebrate the solemnity of the Mass bearing a vast number of wax lights; and no one enters any public place in the city without a taper in his hand".

St. Bernard also (AD 1153) gives the following description of the practice of his own day:-

> We go in procession, two by two, carrying candles in our hands which are lighted, not at a common fire, but at a fire first blessed in the church by a Bishop. They that go out first return last; and in the way we sing, "Great is the Glory of the Lord". We go two by two in commendation of charity and a social life; for so our Saviour sent out his disciples. We carry lights in our hands; first to signify that our light should shine before men; secondly, this we do this day especially in memory of the Wise Virgins (Matt. 25.7) (of whom the blessed Virgin is the chief) that went to meet their Lord with their lamps lit and burning. And from this usage and the many lights set up in the church this day, it is called *Candelaria* or *Candlemas*. Because our works should be all done in the holy fire of charity, therefore the candles are lit with holy fire. They that go out first return last, to teach humility, "in honour preferring one another" (Romans 12.10). Because God loveth a cheerful giver (II Corinthians 9.7), therefore we sing in the way. The procession itself is to teach us that we should not stand idle in the way of life, but go from strength to strength, not looking back to that which is behind, but reaching forward to that which is before (Philippians 3.13).

The festival is placed at 40 days distance from Christmas as that was the interval directed by the law between the day of birth and the day when the mother presented herself for readmission to the congregation and her infant son for an offering to the Lord (Lev. 12.4). It was on this occasion, as we have already noticed, that Simeon gave to the church the *Nunc Dimittis*, in which he proclaimed the glorious and universal Epiphany of the Holy Child when he prophesied of him as "a light to lighten the Gentiles and the glory of God's people Israel". It was then also that the Virgin Mary first learned that sorrow as well as joy was in the wonderful lot assigned her: "Yet a sword shall pierce through your own soul also" (Luke 2.35).

"In the price of redemption (the representative sacrifice offered in the early dawn of the Holy Child's life, to be followed by a more perfect sacrifice in its eventide) it has been noticed that there was a typical meaning, now for the first and only time finding its true signification. The two turtle-doves or young pigeons, were expressive of lowliness at all times as offerings of the poor; but in the offering of one by fire and the eating of the other by the priest, or those who offered it, are now to be seen as a type of Christ offering Himself for sin and also giving Himself to be the spiritual food and sustenance of His people." These words are taken from J H Blunt's *The Annotated Book of Common Prayer*.

So it is when the Christian offers himself in worship. In penitence he seeks the burning up and destruction of all in him that offends; he seeks God's blessing upon all that is good, that it may be of use and value in His service.

If the image of light finds its perfect expression in the light which is Christ, so Christians are to shine as lights in the world, reflecting in their lives the perfect light of their master. This is in no circumstance a light to be hid, but "put... on the stand; it shineth on all that are in the house" (Matt 5.15).

The symbolism of Candlemas is taken up in the ceremonies of the Easter Vigil, when the Light of Christ is proclaimed and all the worshippers again carry candles.

It is also now included in the Anglican rite of Baptism — as too in that of other denominations — when each candidate or his/her representative is given a lighted candle "to show that you have passed from darkness to light; shine as a light in the world to the glory of God the Father".

The Purification of our Lady and the Presentation of her son must indeed constitute a mystery of the faith. In seeking to unveil a tiny corner of the mystery I hope we may have seen that it is also a joyful mystery.

The last of the Joyful Mysteries is the Finding of the Child Jesus in the Temple.

The glory of the Lord was manifested in the Temple when he was 40 days old. It was so again when he was 12 years old, and his presence there on the second occasion was in very different circumstances. On the first he was carried there by his mother. On the second she and her husband Joseph "sought him sorrowing". On the first occasion his glory was revealed only to the faithful souls who "waited for the loving-kindness of the Lord in the midst of his temple". Twelve years later the childhood of the Holy Child was to reveal the same glory to all who had the faith to behold it, during that time when he sat among the doctors and fulfilled the words, "I have more understanding than my teachers" (Psalm 119.99). Among those teachers may have been Nicodemus and Gamaliel. Nicodemus received the first full revelation of the truth about new birth into Christ (John 3.1-8) and Gamaliel became the teacher of St. Paul by whom the light of Christ was spread among the Gentiles (Acts 22.3).

The Joyful Mysteries give place to the Sorrowful Mysteries and they in turn to the Glorious Mysteries and we shall so ponder the events which are thus described. But may we divert for a moment to consider what, according to the Roman Breviary, are listed as the "Seven Sorrows of the Blessed Virgin Mary"? Seven is a number of great significance to Christians. There are seven Corporal Acts of Mercy and Seven Spiritual Acts; Seven Deadly Sins and Seven Cardinal Virtues. There are Seven Gifts of the Holy Ghost and Seven Words from the

Cross; Seven Sacraments and Seven Penitential Psalms. The Seven Sorrows of our Lady are:

(i) The prophecy of Simeon
(ii) The flight into Egypt
(iii) The loss of the Holy Child
(iv) The meeting on the way to Calvary
(v) The standing at the foot of the Cross
(vi) The taking down from the Cross
(vii) The burial

One of the Joyful Mysteries is also the third of the Sorrows of our Lady. The Loss and the Finding of the Holy Child are of course separate events, but in the same story. They serve as a reminder of the endless paradox of the Christian Faith with its close proximity of joy and sorrow. There could not have been the joy of the finding of Jesus if there had not first been the sorrow of discovering him missing. Not only that, we have to ask ourselves, was the sorrow really necessary? As the story stands, Jesus justified his behaviour by claiming a higher obedience than that which he owed to his mother and St Joseph (referred to as 'your father'). It was, he says, his duty to be in his (true) Father's house. Joseph was not his true father, Nazareth not his true house.

Expositors and preachers have wrestled to reconcile his behaviour with the perfection of his nature as they understood it. He certainly inflicted sorrow upon Joseph and Mary. Could he have asserted what he did assert in some other way? The incarnation surely means that he was truly human as well as divine; his boyhood behaviour was truly reprehensible and that fact should not and need not be denied. On his return to Nazareth, St Luke makes a point of his being subject to his human parents — and adds that he "increased in wisdom and stature" (Luke 2.51-52).

There is a difference between sinfulness and imperfection. The human nature of our Lord Jesus Christ was not sinful but it was certainly not "perfect" from the start. We read, "It became Him for whom are all things, and by whom are all things in bringing many sons to glory, to make the captain of their salvation perfect through suffering" (Hebrews 2.10). Again, "Behold I cast out devils and do cures today and tomorrow and the third day I shall be perfected" (Luke 13.32). "Though he were a son yet learned he obedience" (Hebrews 5.8). And in the context, "Jesus increased..." So Jesus was natural; he grew in strength, in wisdom and in grace in the same ways as every other human being could grow and is meant to grow. The halo by which he is so often distinguished in pictures and stained glass was not there in the days of his life on earth. This unique story of his boyhood tells us but little about his early development. What it tells is all the more valuable — for our understanding both of him and of ourselves.

We may first note his patience, implicit in this story because it is all that is recorded of him for the first thirty years of his life. His patience is to know his hour. St. John tells us of three occasions after his ministry had begun, when what he did, or did not do, depended upon the fact that he knew that "his hour had not yet come". (John 2.4; 7.30; 8.20) These are all to be contrasted with the moment (John 13.1) when he knew that his hour had come — and the Passion Narrative begins in the Upper Room. But for thirty years he knew that his hour was not yet and he patiently waited — and grew.

Patience is a virtue indeed and we need every reminder of it to curb our impetuosity and rashness. Yet paradoxically again, impatience can sometimes be an even greater virtue, simply because it is the appropriate and healthy response. In my ministry to people in hospital — who are, significantly, dubbed "patients" — I have often been able to reassure those who are feeling *im*patient that this is probably the right response, after a period when the reverse was true, and it marks the progress made. Indeed impatience can be a tremendous spur to recovery. Our Lord's development in strength was as equally spiritual as physical. We know it from the spiritual maturity which we behold as soon as his ministry begins. In the thirty years of his waiting, he grew to be the strong man of the Gospel and of the Passion. He grew too in wisdom — the wisdom by which he knew and recognised "his hour". But the Gospels tell us of his temptations at the outset of his ministry and of the wisdom by which he was able both to handle them and to learn from them. In the story of his encounter with the doctors we see him hearing and asking. We need not doubt that our Lord grew in wisdom because of his willingness and ability to enquire and to listen, to God, to his parents, as well as to others of whom the rabbis of the story were an example.

He grew in grace. Grace is difficult to define. It is closely related to holiness and therefore, to health and wholeness. It has to do with the harmony of body, mind and spirit. They are full of grace who find mind and emotion in perfect equilibrium in the love and service of God. "The grace of our Lord Jesus Christ" must, after the Lord's prayer, be the most oft repeated of all petitions. St Paul (II Cor. 13.14) gave us this in praying it for the Church in Corinth. He joins grace with love and fellowship as an indivisible trinity. In attributing grace to our Lord, love to the Father and fellowship to the Holy Spirit we may learn something of how St Paul neither "confounded the persons nor divided the substance" of God the Holy Trinity. Our experience of God as we experience Him as Christians, is in fellowship with Him and one another. We learn of His love and respond with our own — and there is the Grace, the Holiness, which Christ knew in its perfection and imparts to us as we both seek and find it.

The finding of the child Jesus is a simple, human story, at first sight, devoid of all mystery. But at its heart lies mystery indeed, and that mystery is best appreciated and most clearly understood when encountered with the same joyful relief which belonged to St. Mary and St. Joseph when they "found that which they had lost".

(b) The Sorrowful Mysteries

If it seems obvious in a book about joy to write about the
Joyful Mysteries of our faith, it may seem inappropriate also
to write about the Sorrowful Mysteries. Surely they belong
to a quite different area of concern. But just as the Joys are
tinged with sorrow, so there is a kind of joy in the Sorrows too.

In the traditional carol *Joys seven*, which focus on the joys
of our Lady, the sixth runs:

To see her own son Jesus Christ
Upon the crucifix.

Here is paradox at its ultimate. How could his mother have
experienced anything remotely resembling joy at the sight of
her son's passion and cruel death? More immediately, how
are we to experience joy at the contemplation of this mystery
and is it appropriate to do so? A consideration of all five
episodes which are listed undeer the heading of the Sorrowful
Mysteries may not after all be inappropriate. But first let us
pause to consider those of the 'Joys Seven' which are not listed
among the mysteries. They are the healing of the lame and
the blind, the raising of the dead, and the reading of the Bible.
Some versions of the carol include the Harrowing of Hell,
which also merits a brief consideration.

The miracles of the healing of the lame and the blind are
examples of the wide range of healings which are attributed
to the ministry of our Lord. They are integral to the Gospel,
with all the other signs and wonders. To expunge them from
the Gospels is to leave very little. They are not in any sense
"added extras". They constitute a major and indivisible part
of what the incarnate life was all about. Attempts have been
made to demythologize the miracles with all else that does
not belong to a so-called modern and scientific rationale. But
it is not a Christianity in any meaningful sense that is left
behind when this is done. We cannot explain the miracles;
they are 'signs' and 'wonders' which leave us marvelling.

More immediately, we ask, Why do such miracles not

happen today? Some maintain that they do, since Jesus is the same yesterday, today and for ever (Heb. 13.8) we must expect him to heal the sick now as he did then. There is some evidence that he does. Unaccountable, sudden and spectacular cures are recorded. Whether the recipients are also healed, in the wider sense of the word, may be another matter. But people can be cured without being healed and healed without being cured. The problem for those who do believe in modern miracles of this sort is that they do not often happen. The way out then is to suggest that the cures are frustrated by human sin or lack of faith. Yet often it is the most deeply penitent who are not cured (cf St Paul and his 'thorn in the flesh': II Cor. 12.7). And if faith the size of a grain of mustard seed can move mountains (Matt. 17.20) it is difficult to see how adequacy of faith can be the missing factor.

Another theory is that the miracles of the Gospel and the rest of the New Testament belong to a particular period of history and were given to evoke faith in the beholders (John 2.11). Once faith had been established the signs were no longer necessary — indeed would have been an impediment to faith (properly contrasted not with unbelief but with sight: Hebrews 11.1)). So God withdrew the miraculous activity once the church was established.

The miracles are mysteries then, and certainly joyful ones. Our intellectual problems must not be brushed aside, but neither must our capacity for wonder be frustrated by them. The healing miracles tell of God's love and compassion and we rejoice to know that these are His eternal characteristics however He does or does not manifest them.

The raising of the dead is in a different category from the miracles of healing. Before his own resurrection, our Lord restored to life Jairus's daughter (Luke 8.49-56), the widow's son at Nain (Luke 7.14-15) and Lazarus (John 11.1-44). There is no doubt that the Evangelists believed and wanted their readers to believe that in every case the death and resurrection were real. It is very rare, as compared with the healing ministry and its cures, that claims are made for the church to have continued to restore the dead to life. In consequence there is normally within the churches' ministry no such expectation. Whatever is believed about the historicity of the events described, we read them now as allegories, of passing, in Christ, from death to life, just as we pass from darkness to light.

The reading of the Bible by our Lord is instanced publicly only once (Luke 4.17). But his knowledge of the Scriptures is evidenced on many occasions. His discovery in the Temple, hearing the doctors and asking them questions suggests a knowledge of the Law. We need not here instance all the references which bear testimony to his knowledge. We follow his example immensely the richer for having at our disposal not only the Old Testament but the New. Written for our learning we still pray that we may "so read, mark, learn and inwardly digest them that by patience, and the comfort of his holy word, we may embrace and ever hold fast the blessed hope of everlasting life given us in our Saviour Jesus Christ". (Collect for Advent II, Book of Common Prayer.)

The Harrowing of Hell, sometimes added to the 'Joys Seven', is the medieval English term for the defeat of the power of evil at the Descent of Christ into 'Hell' after his death. It was a favourite theme of art and drama in the Middle Ages. 'Hell' is used here not in the ultimate sense of final separation from God, but to the realm of existence which is neither heaven nor hell but a place or state where the souls of pre-Christian people waited for the message of the Gospel and whither went the penitent thief after his death on the cross (Luke 23.43). To believe in the retrospective power of Christ's atoning work is surely right and proper however we conceptualise it. The concept of the harrowing of hell may not be Biblical in the strict sense (though consider Matt. 27.5; Luke 23.43; 1 Peter 3.18-20) but it is a poetic phrase which does justice to the belief of many Christians about the hereafter.

We turn now to the Agony and Prayer in the Garden.

We cannot know precisely what our Lord was experiencing in the time of agony but we are not being merely fanciful, still less detracting from the reality of the suffering, by surmising that there was some sense of achievement and satisfaction when the moment of "no return" was reached and passed. The agony is the end of the beginning and the beginning of the end. The *Tetolesti* ("it is finished") of the cross was in a real sense already his to proclaim when he reached this point. It is an essential part of our belief that Christ "laid down his life". It was not taken from him (John 10.14-18). It was in Gethsemane that the final decision was made, and the totality of his submission to the will of the Father made manifest. If there was agony in the doubt which his prayer there suggests, must there not have been joy when the doubt was resolved and he knew there was only one way forward?

All too often Christians have thought that the purpose of meditating upon the Passion is to evoke our pity. Faber in his passiontide hymn wrote "O come and mourn with me awhile" (Ancient and Modern 113) but on the Via Dolorosa our Lord rebuked the women of Jerusalem: "Weep not for me but weep for yourselves and for your children" (Luke 23.2). It is not to pity but to penitence that we are to be moved and to a share in the joy which his atoning work has made possible, our reconciliation to God.

As we meditate upon the mystery then, we find joy in Christ's submission and are moved to make our own submission to the will of God both greater and more joyful. Moreover we learn that it is not always the will of the Father to free us from pain or save us from sorrow of mind or spirit. In a sinful world, made so by our misuse of His gift of free will, it is often only through suffering that His will can be achieved. We are right to pray for deliverance — that is a natural desire. We are right to pray "thy will be done", not as a doleful submission but as a cry of victory over defeat.

It is not my intention to dwell for long on the scourging and crowning with thorns, two terrible acts of torture so much more likely to occasion us sorrow than joy. Torture and death are still meted out to countless men and women in a great many parts of the world. Some, but very few, have found consolation in coupling this agony with that of their Lord. The only possible joy for our Lord himself would have been in his triumph over both physical and mental torture, his integrity unimpaired. All the Evangelists refer to the scourging and to the mocking of Jesus, but they do so not to harrow our feelings but to point to the dignity with which he bore them. He is ever our example and the source of our courage in the face of such adversities which may come our way. For most of us physical and mental torment, on account of our faith, rarely if ever arise. For this we are, quite properly, thankful. Some of course do suffer the extremes of physical and mental pain, involuntarily and occasioned by circumstances quite beyond their control. The circumstances of their agony may be very different from those who are martyrs to a faith or a cause, but we are all greatly impressed when the response to it is one of patient and dignified acceptance. Their example is indeed a source of admiration, and, dare we say, of joy. So we turn to the two remaining mysteries — the carrying of the cross and the crucifixion.

"Strong enough to carry a man and light enough for a man to carry" — so the nature of the barbaric and cruel means of execution was described. Prisoners carried their crosses, literally, to the place of execution and in doing so have given us a metaphor for the bearing of our own sorrows.

Joy may come from a more profound understanding of the Passion than is commonly ours. Suppose one is reading the story for the first time, or imagine one's self viewing a painting of the scene, for the first time. The heading to the story, the title of the picture, must be "Defeat" or "Black Friday", we would suppose. But we find it entitled "Victory" or "Good Friday", and we look for the explanation of the paradox. A reading of the Passiontide hymn of Bishop Fortunatus might be our clue (Ancient and Modern, Revised, 97)

Sing, my tongue, the glorious battle
    Sing the last, the dread affray;
O'er the Cross, the Victor's trophy
    Sound the high triumphal lay,
How the pains of death enduring
    Earth's Redeemer won the day.
Faithful Cross above all other,
    One and only noble Tree;
None in foliage, none in blossom,
    None in fruit thy peer may be;
Sweet the wood and sweet the iron
    And thy load, most sweet is he.

To read the Gospels is to read our Lord's proclamation of the advent of his Father's kingdom. It is to read of his sublime teaching and his great works of mercy. It is to see lips consecrated to the service of his Father and the blessing of all who heard him. It is to see his journeying on his errands of healing and saving; it is to see his hands outstretched to bless.

To read the Passion story is to see the same Jesus robbed of all these powers, his hands and feet nailed to a cross, his lips capable of wonderful words but now very few, and not for long. His heart is literally pierced by a soldier's spear as metaphorically his own heart is broken at the hardness of the hearts of all around him.

And yet, his greatest work is achieved not in the opening stories of the Gospel, but in his Passion and his Death. They seem to spell disaster, but in fact spell victory.

To approach the Passion story in that light-hearted way which the word joy may suggest would seem to many to be wholly inappropriate. In a sense, it would. Yet in the most profound of ways, it is a source of incredible and unequalled joy — the joy of creation renewed. The joy of the new creation is made possible by it. What the Garden of Eden was in our creation, Calvary is in our salvation.

Here might I stay and sing
No story so divine;
Never was love, dear King,
Never was grief like thine.
This is my friend,
In whose sweet praise
I all my days
Could gladly spend.

(S Crossman)

The emphasis of the Western Church on the crucifixion needs to be balanced by the Eastern emphasis on Christ in Glory. In the dome of an Orthodox Church the Pantokraton, Christ the Lord of all, is portrayed. We can find joy in the passion of our Lord only because we know it was not the end of the story.

So central to Christianity is the death and the resurrection of the Lord that every Friday is seen as a weekly reminder of Good Friday, and observed as a day of abstinence, and every Sunday as a little Easter. Christians do not keep the Sabbath (Seventh) Day, but Sunday — the first day — because it was the day of the resurrection. Fasting and abstinence are out of fashion, but the practice of some such discipline on Fridays could only help to keep us mindful of the passion. Likewise keeping Sunday holy — separate and different and an occasion for worship — is not to make it wearisome and spoil-sport, but an occasion for the rekindling of joy and delight — a celebration.

What we seem to have lost is the capacity to identify. In the secular world of everyday life this is not so at all. My son Richard, as a little boy, used to revel in the TV series "The man from Uncle". Before each episode he would go to his "Uncle cupboard" and dress himself with hat, and belt and gun, to identify with his hero. My grandson Tom wears the colours and motifs of his favourite football team when he goes to see Coventry City play. The identification is deep and meaningful. But how do we, and how do we teach our children and grandchildren, to identify with Jesus? Keeping Fridays and Sundays each week, and the major Festivals year by year must of course help. But the identification really depends upon a shared concern, minding about the things that Jesus minded about and making him real in their everyday lives as well as on Sundays. If the resurrection is the focus of joy and glory in the incarnate life it is so only because it was the focus of joy and glory in the life of Christ's disciples. They wrote and proclaimed his healing and saving Gospel, that it might become the Gospel of joy and glory for every successive generation of Christians.

In this study we put the Annunciation and the Nativity before the Resurrection. But strictly speaking we should begin with the Resurrection and work backwards and forwards from it. That is to begin with the Glory and then to see its origin — and its cost! If we identify with Christ's glory, we shall more easily identify with all else that he was, and said and did — and is. When the Psalmist proclaimed

I was glad when they said unto me,
"Let us go into the house of the Lord".

(Psalm 122.1)

he was stating what he actually experienced — joy and pleasure in his worship. If this is not our experience too it will not be long before we abandon our worship. We shall be identifying with a false image and our loss will be little if we abandon it. Indeed it may be our gain. The 'happy, clappy' way of worship may fill us with dismay if not horror, but it calls attention to an essential element of our worship, that we should enjoy it, revel in it, find it an occasion for spiritual revival.

How often has it been said to me as I have shaken hands with people at the church door, "Rector, I did enjoy the service" and then "But perhaps I shouldn't say enjoy". So deeply affected are we all by the kill-joy spirit of Puritanism that we can actually feel guilty when we enjoy an act of worship! Those who have responsibility for devising liturgy and leading worship must make sure that solemnity does not banish joy and give to the word "celebrate" the emphasis on "singing to the Lord with cheerful voice" which is inseparable from its true understanding.

(c) The Glorious Mysteries

We turn now to the so called Glorious Mysteries, which set the seal on the victory of the cross. They are the ultimate source of joy to the church in every age. They were such a source to the original disciples. The disciples experienced them against the background of defeat and utter desolation — their natural response to the mysteries of the passion.

Of these five mysteries, three are scriptural and two are not. There is no evidence of the bodily assumption of our Lady or of her coronation. Because they are not recorded in scripture Christians who believe in them do so on the authority of the church, or of that part of it to which they belong. They may believe in them as mysteries which enshrine truths, mysterious and inexplicable yet worthy of the kind of credence given to the creation stories in the book of Genesis. It is no part of this little book to lay claim to dogmatic theology nor is it my purpose to be deliberately controversial. I shall comment on the final two mysteries only to emphasise truths which I believe to be important for all of us on our spiritual journey and which do not depend upon the assumption and coronation being historically true or in the same category as the resurrection and ascension of our Lord and the descent of the Holy Spirit.

68

We turn then first to the resurrection of our Lord.

In his first epistle to the Corinthians (15.17-19) St Paul wrote: "If Christ be not raised your faith is vain; ye are yet in your sins. Then they also which are fallen asleep in Christ are perished. If in this life only we have hope in Christ, we are of all men most miserable."

All four Gospels record the Resurrection and it has been, and is, an article of faith for all Christian people. But it is rightly called a Mystery. It is not, as Dr David Jenkins, until recently Bishop of Durham, has so rightly said, a "conjuring trick with bones". Our Lord's resurrection can only be compared and contrasted with the raising of Jairus's daughter or of Lazarus. They came to life again, and would eventually die again. For them there was no Ascension! Our Lord's resurrection was not a resumption of the *status quo ante*. He appeared to his disciples as evident proof that he was alive but he was unidentified by those who knew him on his journey to Emmaus (Luke 24.13-31) and "vanished out of their sight". He appeared to his disciples in a room the door of which was locked (John 20.26).

Scripture makes it perfectly plain that the Lord was alive again, and equally clear that he was not in the same mode of life, or in the same kind of relationship with his followers as he had been before. It is for these reasons that we think of the resurrection as a mystery as well as a miracle. Miracle, because the Church has always been moved to wonder; mystery, because the event is past human understanding.

Yet it remains the source of joy beyond all others. The Resurrection is to the Nativity what the completion of any task is to its beginning. If Christmas marks the beginning of the incarnate life of our Lord and is called a joyful mystery, so Easter marks the ultimate and victorious conclusion of what was then begun. If Christ's glory was laid aside in the manger, it is supremely revealed in the resurrection appearances.

The fact of the resurrection is not self-evident. Our Lord did not triumph over his enemies in a worldly sense. We must never lose sight of the truth that he laid down his life — it was not taken from him. He triumphed over death, not over those who put him to death. Easter does not reverse Good Friday; it confirms the victory which took place on the cross. Our Lord's resurrection appearances required faith in the beholders — and still do of us. We cannot rationalise it, or explain it. Our belief in it does not depend upon our doing so.

Our faith is indeed vain if there is no objective reality in the resurrection of Jesus. Our own hope of life after death is assured by it.

> Jesus lives! henceforth is death
> But the gate of life immortal

The Christian views his own certain end in the light of the resurrection and the hope that it brings. If when every hope on earth is disappointed, as may and does happen to a great many people, if then there is only death and nothingness beyond, misery is indeed their lot. But if the ultimate hope, of heaven and the vision of God is guaranteed by the rising again of our Lord, then disappointment and the dashing of hopes may indeed be painful but are not ultimate disaster. Many who seek the church's ministry of healing are in great need of a remedy for their lack of hope and sense of hopelessness. We have a pearl of great price to offer — the promises which stem from the passion, death and resurrection of our Lord. The glorious mystery of the resurrection is the greatest source of joy the world has ever known. Our failure, the church's failure, to proclaim it is highly irresponsible and infinitely cruel. Yet we are, as I have already observed, constantly told that when we counsel those who come to us with their problems we must not introduce the subject of religion unless they do. We are warned against using the counselling situation to evangelise. We are told of the dangers of trying to "force religion down people's throats". But when the doctor prescribes what he believes will help or even cure his patient, he does not compel the patient to take it! The freedom of the patient, the client, every man and woman,

70

to go his or her own way is God's gift to us all, and all of us must respect that freedom for others as we guard it for ourselves. Of course! But to evangelise, properly understood, is to communicate good news. The resurrection of our Lord is good news. The joy of those who believe in it is good news. A glorious mystery is one in which we glory! Glory is the subjective side of which mystery is the objective. If we give thanks as we do, or ought, for those who brought us to faith, how can we not be faithful to the charge of bringing others to faith and hope, to joy and glory?

The second of the Glorious Mysteries is the Ascension of our Lord Jesus Christ.

St Luke begins his Gospel with a note of joy — and ends it likewise. As our Lord ascended into the heavens he blessed his disciples and "they worshipped him and returned to Jerusalem with great joy". In his second volume, the Acts of the Apostles, Luke records the switch from Jew to Gentile as the recipients of Paul's ministry and message and remarks that even as the disciples were banished from Iconium

they were filled with joy
and with the Holy Ghost.

(Acts 13.52)

It is almost impossible to read the verse without understanding it as saying that joy and the Holy Ghost are to all intents synonyms. Where the Spirit of God is, there is joy. Where there is joy, the Spirit cannot be far distant. St Paul (Romans 15.13) wrote in similar vein to the Romans when he blessed his readers with the words:

Now the God of hope fill you will all joy and peace
in believing, that ye may abound in hope through
the power of the Holy Ghost.

His Philippian convert he described as "dearly beloved and longed for, my joy and crown."

If the Gospel we preach and proclaim is not joyful it is not the Gospel. So we turn now to the Ascension.

The Ascension is part of the Easter story. It is normally

celebrated on the 40th day of Easter, the assumed period of the resurrection appearances (Acts 1.3). St. Luke who testifies to the Ascension both in his Gospel and in the Book of the Acts describes how the Apostle "looked steadfastly towards heaven as he went up". Two men, two angels, appeared to them and said, "Ye men of Galilee why stand ye gazing up into heaven?"

Yet the stance which was theirs then has been and will be the stance of Christian believers, always. Once the church ceases to gaze up into heaven, it loses its inspiration and its worship dries up. Again we are confronted with paradox. In the Acts of the Apostles, they return to Jerusalem after the Ascension to pray and to plan. The church incarnates God today as has been its mission from the beginning. Its concern is the world. Its mission is to all human kind. It is to be involved at every point of human life and experience — and it is to look up, to gaze and wonder at the things of heaven, so that the Kingdom of Heaven may be established upon earth.

I believe it was Charles Spurgeon, the great Baptist preacher (1834-1892), who said, "When you speak of Heaven, your whole face should light up; when you speak of Hell — well, your usual face will do". We are not meant to be citizens of heaven only when we are in an attitude of prayer or worship. Our Lord and those chosen apostles Peter, James and John, shared a mystical, numinous experience, on the Mount of Transfiguration. They came down from the mountain to engage in a healing ministry of some difficulty and complexity. I was helped by a very simple analogy related in a sermon that I heard. It compared the Christian life to a dancing class. If you look down at your feet, you will trip, and tread on those of your partner. If you look up, your feet will look after themselves. We have all heard of people who are "so heavenly minded as to be of no earthly use". Solving the paradox in that way is just as reprehensible as it is to have only Gospel, concerned with the here and now of this-worldly activity.

It is when we seek to hold the two aspects together that we arrive at the truth and the Kingdom of Heaven is realised among us.

The truth is beautifully summed up in the *Book of Common Prayer* collect for the Ascension:

> Grant we beseech thee Almighty God, that like as
> we do believe thy only-begotten Son our Lord Jesus
> Christ to have ascended into the heavens; so may we
> also in heart and mind thither ascend and with him
> continually dwell.

The ascension is a mystery. Those who believe that the resurrection body of our Lord was exactly the body which was nailed to the cross, and unchanged, disappeared into the clouds, have then such awkward — and silly — questions to answer as "What does he do for food?" I think it was Dr. Chadwick who said: "When we say that Jesus is seated *on* God's right hand, we do not believe it literally". Speculation about what really happened to the physical body of Jesus is, of course, natural and in no way improper, but it can never lead to a conclusion which really amounts to an explanation. This is the difference between a problem and a mystery, in the sense in which mystery is here used. Problems admit of solutions which may or may not be forthcoming. Mysteries admit of no solution. They are, as it were, by definition beyond our comprehension. They demand of us a totally different kind of response — of wonder, love and praise. This response depends upon faith — which is itself a mystery. To those who have faith, the Ascension is the conclusion of the Resurrection appearances and gives rise not only to a belief in an admittedly inexplicable event, but also to a belief in a present reality: — Jesus lives. He lives "in heaven" seated on the right hand of the Father. He lives in the church, the "colony" of heaven on earth. He lives in the hearts of all faithful people, who acknowledge him and call upon his name. I believe that he lives also in the hearts of all who seek to know and love God, even though by them he is not named. Canon Eric James once paraphrased John Keble's verse in his hymn "When God of old came down from Heaven (AMR 154). In verse 6 Keble wrote,

> Only in stubborn hearts and wills
>> No place for it is found.

"It" refers to the Holy Spirit and Eric James suggested:

> Even in stubborn hearts and wills
>> Some place for it is found.

The seeking of definition where none is really to be found often leads to a serious narrowing of our understanding and an exclusiveness which is totally incompatible with our Lord's own words,

> "I, if I be lifted up from the earth, will draw all men unto me".

Our Lord was referring to his crucifixion. The cross indeed draws us to him, so does his resurrection and so does his Ascension, because it is he who draws us, and draws not *some* but *all* men.

The next of the Glorious Mysteries is the Descent of the Holy Spirit, to which we now turn.

The gifts of the Holy Spirit are the ingredients of heaven. When we have them on earth, the Kingdom of Heaven is within us. They are the qualities of life which span the divide between earth and heaven, the qualities we take with us on our journey thither. But the qualities are not separable from him whose gifts they are. Joy is a gift of the Spirit. Joy is the Spirit.

When on earth in the ordinary course of human life and experience we give and receive gifts, it is easy to separate the gifts from the giver — or so at first it seems. Canon Graham Smallwood tells the story of his wife saying to their little son, when she was writing to her husband, "Would you like to send Daddy your love?" He thought for a moment and replied: "Yes, but how do I get it out of me and into the envelope?" No doubt his mother's hand guided him as he put a kiss at the bottom of the letter — and it was done. We do in fact value the gifts we receive all the more if they, in a real sense, come "with love from", that is, represent the giver. Sometimes we have received a gift from someone from whom we would rather not have received it. It does not represent the relationship as we perceive it.

In the Jewish sacrificial system the offerings were always seen as vicarious, as representative of the giver, who laid his hand upon the sacrificial lamb to identify himself with it. In our Eucharistic worship we give the bread and wine to the priest and as we do so we offer ourselves, our life, our work, all that we have and are. The gifts on the altar represent us. *we* are on the altar. And just as the bread and wine become the vehicles of Christ's presence, his body and his blood, so our lives are transformed by his healing, saving, consecrating touch. The gift and the giver are inseparable in both directions. We give ourselves under the token of bread and wine; Christ gives himself under the token of his body and blood.

So the gifts of the Holy Spirit are not to be separated from the giver. We have the gifts only when we have the giver. As our hearts are open to him so we experience the love, the joy and the peace, the constituent 'parts' of the Holy Spirit of God.

How does he 'descend'? We must never confuse the imagery with the reality. Bishop John Robinson taught us that God is in the depth of our being. To look into the depths is to look down and not up! Both images are true. God is in His heaven. He is the creator. He is separate from and different from his creation.

Holy, Holy, Holy! Though the darkness hide thee
   Though the eye of sinful man thy glory may not see
   Only thou art holy, there is none beside thee
   Perfect in power, in love and purity. (AMR 160)

We sing these words, but the spirit of reverence and fear is often missing. We "pop into church". We do not, as it were, "take off our shoes because the place whereon we stand is holy ground" (Exodus 3.5). We worship God in "an orgy of matiness" rather than "the beauty of holiness". God's transcendence, His infinite glory, requires of us a response we all too rarely consider. And why? Because the obverse of the coin is also true, but it must be held alongside not instead of the transcendent. We call it the immanent, God with us, and we are at home in our Father's house, familiar as children are with a loving parent. So we look down and find that the Spirit of the living God is indeed the ground of our very being — the creator Spirit creating us now, and we depending wholly upon his presence. But we also look up and away, and catch glimpses when we may of the God who, were we to see Him, would destroy us (Exodus 24.16).

This is a book about joy and this gives us our focus on the Holy Spirit. The Spirit teaches us to acknowledge both the glory of God and the immediacy of His presence. Joy is our experience in every case. When worship is offered in the beauty of an ancient cathedral, art and architecture capturing our vision and speaking to us of God; when beautiful music and superb ceremonial lift our hearts and minds to God in glory; when the Holy Spirit enlivens our senses and quickens our love for God, our maker and redeemer; when these things happen, we are indeed lost in wonder, love and praise. The word ecstacy comes from the Latin and means "to stand outside". We are "beside ourselves", "lost" indeed, with a joy we can often only express in song, if indeed it is not ineffable, beyond all expression.

But our worship may be in a very different context, or we may be simply at prayer in our own room. His presence we experience at quite another level; he is with us as friend; we talk and we listen, we are still and know that He is God — not in heaven but on earth. Earth of course then becomes heaven for us and our joy is complete.

Books in number have of course been written about the Holy Spirit. In writing of the Spirit under the heading of a Glorious Mystery, I am emphasising both the glory in which we have part and the mystery which reminds us of the very finite nature of our understanding. Man does not understand himself — how shall he understand God? When St. Augustine wrote his treatise on the Trinity (*De Trinitate*) he had a vision of himself walking along the sea shore. He saw a child scooping water with a shell, from the sea into a hole he had made in the sand. "Look", he said to the child, "at the vastness of the ocean and littleness of the hole you have made!" The child turned into an angel and said, "Look at the size of your human mind in which you seek to enclose God Himself".

The fourth of the Glorious Mysteries is The Assumption of the Blessed Virgin Mary. Let us first consider a historical note.

The doctrine of the assumption was not defined until 1950 when Pope Pius XII did so, and provided a new mass for the Feast. But this was after a long history. The first references date back to the 4th century and refer to the death of the Blessed Virgin Mary at Jerusalem and to her bodily assumption either immediately or after three days. In the 5th and 6th centuries there are references in both the Eastern and Western Churches and the doctrine was probably first upheld on grounds of deductive theology in an 8th or 9th century letter attributed to St. Augustine, and was later defended by St Albertus Magnus, St Thomas Aquinas and St Bonaventure.

It disappeared from the Anglican Book of Common Prayer in 1549 and has not been officially restored. Under the title *Koimesis* or *Dormition* — the Greek and Latin words for "Falling asleep" — there could be no possible grounds for protest and her departure from this world could be honoured in terms acceptable to all Christian people. In East and West alike the date observed is 15th August.

It is difficult to remember that some of the most traditional doctrines of the church were at one time highly debatable and indeed debated. The argument against the phrase in the

Nicene Creed, which describes our Lord as "being of one substance with the Father" was that it is entirely unscriptural! It was eventually included on the grounds that it expressed as clearly as possible what was covert in the scriptures and became a test of orthodoxy for that reason. Those who profess a belief in the assumption — and coronation — of our Lady do so for the same sort of reason. There is no evidence and no text to support these dogmas, but they are reasonable suppositions in accordance with the credal statements. Christians are divided on the importance of including them in the corpus of Christian belief, and always will be. We are confronted with mysteries and we can only ask, Are the "truths" enshrined implicit in the beliefs we do hold, though not explicit? Do they help us to hold more surely to the essential beliefs? Let us consider this further.

The doctrine of the resurrection of the body means that we are and shall always be men and women and the same men and women that we have always been. A glorified body, a resurrection body is a non-spatial one. As it was with our Lord, so it will be with us. But what of our Lady? Can we envisage a separation of her soul and body? Our Lord's resurrection body, as we have already seen in our consideration of that mystery, was not simply his physical body *redivivus*. It was sown a physical body, it was raised a spiritual body. The intellectual problem of understanding how human beings can exist between death and resurrection "discarnate" is far greater than the difficulty of believing that our Lady knew no such dissolution.

It is one of the most important emphases of the healing ministry that a human being, body, mind and spirit, is an indissoluble trinity, yet at death it would seem that the body is separated from the other two component aspects of our being. Can this be so? Is not the "resurrection body" already ours at death? We do not know. We cannot know. But we can keep our minds open and ensure that our capacity for wonder at mysteries beyond our probing is not stultified by preconceived negations. What all Christians surely want to do is to rejoice in the fullness of our Lady's joy. We want to, because we recognise her as the mother of the new creation, the enabler of the Word becoming flesh, the *sine qua non* of our salvation. She is, when all is said and done, *our* lady.

The last of the Glorious Mysteries is The Coronation of the Blessed Virgin Mary.

In the Roman Catholic Church, there is observed on August 2nd the Feast of the Queenship of Mary. Her Coronation is not a dogma; it is however, like the dogma of the Assumption, based on deductive theology and the concept of Mary as the Queen of Heaven, crowned as such by her son has obvious devotional appeal, even though it is based on art and poetry, rather than history. Certainly many believe that she is the one complete human person in heaven and honour her as such. Coronation, queenship — these are images drawn from human, this-worldly concepts. They may seem less and less relevant in a world where monarchies grow fewer. The concept of a republic does not provide a comparable imagery. In Great Britain we have a monarchy and a monarch who was crowned. She was crowned because she was Queen not Queen because she was crowned. Whatever role in fact belongs to our Lady, she has it as a consequence of the Annunciation and her willing response to her call. If we celebrate that event, there is logic in keeping the coronation as a "feast of devotion". It is the culmination of a vocation perfectly fulfilled. A mystery? Yes. A glorious mystery and a source of joy to all who contemplate it. It may be fanciful to think of our Lady as being crowned, but no more so than to think of ourselves as also being the recipients of such tokens. Our vocation is to be:

Changed from glory into glory
Till in heaven we take our place
Till we cast our crowns before thee
Lost in wonder, love and praise.

(Charles Wesley, based on Revelation 4.10.)

CHAPTER 5

THE JOY OF GIVING

(a) Of our Resources

Laughter has undoubted therapeutic value in the cure of disease and disorder. It may play an equally important part in the prevention of illness. Joyful people are less likely to become ill than the sorrowful. Joyful people are more likely to turn illness to good effect — to find joy in and through sickness if not from it. We know this almost instinctively and highly revere, for instance, the clown and the comedian in consequence.

Let us remind ourselves that being joyful is part of being healthy, not only a means to it. So we now look at some of the attitudes and dispositions which make for joy. First we consider *giving*, and in particular the giving of our means and our resources.

We are all relatively rich people. If a list could be made of all the people alive in the world today in order of their worldly possessions, we should appear very high indeed in the league. Yes, there would be some ahead of us but countless millions behind us. Let me ask a question of my readers that I have sometimes asked of an audience. "Do you have a bank account?" Ignoring the pence column, what is the last figure, in the pounds column, of your present bank statement? You will be a very exceptional person if you know the answer. The fact therefore is that you could give away up to £10 without even knowing you had done so. Many of us could give away £100 and likewise be ignorant of the fact. It is then salutary to remember, and constantly to remind ourselves, that giving of our resources is our duty and ought to be our joy. The fact is that no-one suffers more from my meanness or gains more from my generosity than I do. The image of Scrooge is known to us all. To be mean is to be miserable. Indeed the very word miserable is derived from the same Latin word *miser*, which means wretched. If a miser is wretched, a generous man is joyful. Our Lord himself is quoted by St Paul as having said: "It is more blessed to give than to receive". Our Lord also drew a strong connection between giving and receiving. We have already quoted two of his admonitions:

"Give, and it shall be given unto you"

"Freely have ye received, freely give".

The needy have never been needier or more numerous than they are today. We as Christians should always be asking ourselves how much can we give — not how little can we get away with giving. Cuthbert Bardsley, sometime Bishop of Coventry used to say, "The last part of a person to be converted is his pocket, her purse". Much as we admire generosity in other people we are often reluctant to practise it much ourselves. William Wordsworth wrote:

Give all thou canst; high Heaven rejects the lore

Of nicely-calculated less or more

(Ecclesiastical Sonnets XI iii)

The Old Testament concept of tithing related to a very different culture from our own, but it remains a valid starting point for our consideration of what we should give. Of course our commitments as well as our resources have to be taken into account. Of course prudence is a cardinal virtue — but it is not a very exciting one. Of course, too, generosity really only begins when we are aware of our giving.

Frank Harvey, the late and still much lamented Archdeacon of London, used to tell this story — against himself. It dates back to the days when we had notes not coins to the value of a pound. As a Canon of St Paul's he would often be in the congregation at 8am on a Sunday morning. He had resolved that a coin in the collection was not good enough — it should be a note. On one Sunday morning he found to his dismay that he had no £1 notes — only a £5 note. He tussled with his conscience as the verger drew near — and gave the £5. "How pleased", he added, "God was with me".

Later that day he was in a public house with a small group of friends. He took their "orders" to the bar — and handed over, without a thought £5.60. It was not, he said, until he said his prayers that night that he considered the differences between those two five pound notes. Do we consider our giving in the context of our spending?

Many years ago a young woman came to be "churched" — the office of thanksgiving after child-birth. When she had gone I found she had left three pence on the plate. It was Denis Duncan who, in a very different context, coined the phrase, "Creative irresponsibility". Could your giving or mine possibly be so described?

In the Church of England it is customary for alms either to be placed in a dish at the back of the church, or to be collected during the singing of a hymn. In either event the act of giving as an act of worship is obscured. Envelope schemes serve more than one purpose, but is one of them to hide our shame at giving so little — or our pride at giving so much? At the end of the service one Sunday, a man protested to his family, as they made their way down the path, how poor was the sermon and how wretched the choir. His little son reminded him that he had often said that you don't get much for £1 these days!

Our giving is or ought to be part of our worship. We offer our gift to God, and ask him to bless it and us, as we do so.

I have singled out money as if it were the only resource but we need all to consider what else we may give to or share with our neighbours. The large house may be made available to others than our immediate family, or the large garden likewise. The car which we find essential for our own needs may still be available to an elderly or infirm — or simply poor — neighbour, for a hospital visit or a shopping expedition. Stewardship has become part of the Christian language recently, in quite new ways. It suggests first and foremost an attitude of mind. "I do not own my resources: I hold them in trust for God".

(b) Of our Time

We are to give of our time directly to God in worship and in prayer and indirectly, as we give it in service of others.

Where time is concerned we are all equal. Whatever the figures on our bank statements, yours and mine, are unlikely to be the same. (I hope, for your sake, that the difference is large!) But we all have 24 hours, every day. Part is to be spent in worship, and fortunate are those whose acts of worship are accompanied by added sources of joy — a beautiful building, wonderful music, a large congregation, inspired preaching: "I was glad when they said unto me, let us go into the house of the Lord". But we are to worship not primarily because we love to do so, but because we love God. The circumstances of our worship may enhance it, but that is just a bonus. The same is true of our prayers. We pray because we love God, not because we like praying (which may or may not be the case).

A man resolved to give God half an hour of prayer each morning. One day everything seemed against him. There was no spark, no joy, no sense or meaning. He was frigid in every way and sorely tempted to give up and get on with "something useful". But he had resolved and he kept to his time. Later on, he was given a vision, a conversation between God and the Devil. The Devil said to God: "You didn't get much out of *that*" to which God replied: "He didn't do it for you, and he certainly didn't do it for himself..." Giving God the time may seem to be all we have to give him sometimes. But if we do so, we are really giving him our wills, and that is so much more important than our feelings. Do we pray and worship only when we feel 'soulful'? Could anything be less generous? But see your praying, private and corporate, as giving to God, see your failure to do so a a refusal to give... You will then have the incentive, the motive to give — and in giving you will receive.

Paradox, seeming contradiction, is often an indication that we are near the truth. "He sees not clearest who sees all things clear" is an aphorism which I have often found helpful. When considering how we should allocate our time we are faced with the dilemma of regularity or spontaneity. The Pharisees are always thought of as having erred in the first of these respects — yet we need rule and order and discipline if our religion is not to be what the late Bishop Walter Carey described as "all bosom and no backbone". It is equally true that if space is not left for the expression of what comes to us spontaneously we shall find that the joy soon goes out of our religion.

An indicator of rule in Christian worship has been expressed as

> The Lord's Service
> in the Lord's House
> for the Lord's People
> on the Lord's Day.

One of the problems of that sort of language is that it implies that what is not designated as "the Lord's" somehow belongs to someone else.

I remember a Sermon many years ago in which the preacher told us of a man who gave up his career as an accountant in order to work "full-time for God", and so to be ordained! We are all meant to be working full-time for God whatever our profession or vocation. Those who do so more explicitly than others do so in order to insist upon that truth. Christians may call themselves "the Lord's People" but only to establish that all people are made by God, in his image and likeness. The Lord's House may be an apt description of a church building, but not if it suggests that all the other houses in the community are not also God's. Dualism creeps into the thinking and attitude of Christian people without their awareness. God is the owner of all things as he is the author of all things. Mrs. Alexander wrote:

All things bright and beautiful
All creatures great and small
All things wise and wonderful
The Lord God made them all.

Yes, but equally truly — and I don't know who wrote it
— is the verse
All things dull and ugly
All things short and squat
All things rude and nasty
The Lord God made the lot.

So the idea of giving to God is itself paradoxical — we can
only give what is already His. "All things come of thee O
Lord And of thine own do we give thee" says the priest as
he blesses the alms. It is equally true of our time as it is of
our means. Our joy in receiving is to be matched by our joy
in surrendering to God and sharing with our fellow creatures.

How often have we excused ourselves from some particular
or on-going act of service with the words: "I would if I had
the time" but do we consider why it is we have so little time
to give away? The pursuit of riches, of power, of comfort is
not wrong in itself, but if it leaves us with no time to give
away, there is surely something wrong. The fact that we cannot
respond to all the claims does not entitle us to respond to none
of them. But the point to be made is that we suffer from this
failure to respond, as well as other people. We are forfeiting
the joy which would be ours if we were more generous.
Gratitude for what we have must be matched by generosity.
A due sense of all God's mercies demands, as the General
Thanksgiving (BCP) has it, that we "show forth his praise,
not only with our lips but in our lives".

St Ignatius Loyola gave us a prayer which has become
widely used and very well known. In it we pray that we may
"labour and not ask for any reward". It is good that we should
serve God for the joy of doing so and not for what we think
we may get out of it. Yet paradoxically again, the Scriptures
constantly promise us rewards. In the 'Angelus' we pray that

we may be "made worthy of the promises of Christ". One has only to read the Beatitudes to read a whole catalogue of promises of reward.

Of course there are times when we just do not feel like giving, when it seems much more a sorrow than a joy. That is why we need discipline and rule — to help us through those times. Then we can say with the Psalmist,

Heaviness may endure for a night
But joy cometh in the morning.

Time and money do not exhaust what we have to give. Let us look at areas which may often be more costly still. When St Paul wrote his hymn to charity (I Cor. 13), he was concerned that we should give not only of our possessions but of our very selves. But if the cost is greater, so also are the rewards and satisfactions.

(c) Of our Interest

The sin of pride is the deadliest of the deadly sins because it enthrones self where God ought to be and ultimately inhibits any concern for any one else. Humility is the greatest of virtues because it is (literally) the ground (*humus*) of all the others and because it puts us in our place. In times of joy and in times of sorrow we, and everyone else, need someone with whom we can share. Sorrow is then ameliorated and joy equally enhanced. One of the evil consequences of the break-up of communities is the isolation and loneliness which it inflicts on many individuals. They have no one with whom to share.

The breakdown of natural communities has required the setting up of 'artificial' ones and however much we lament the cause and occasion we can only rejoice that the response has been made. Will not, for instance, the founding of The Samaritans be regarded, one day, as one of the church's most important pieces of outreach in the century? The huge increase in the number of agencies and individuals offering counselling, befriending and Christian listening is occasioned by people's desperate need to share. If no one takes an interest our joys are no longer joys and our sorrows greatly intensified.

It seems to be less readily recognised that we need people to share in our happiness just as surely as we do our tribulations. This was brought home to me many years ago when I was invited to conduct a Healing Mission in Zimbabwe. At the end of the time I was rewarded with a trip to the Victoria Falls, flight and hotel paid for. It was the experience of a life-time — but the pleasure was greatly diminished because I was all alone!

So we are to be generous with our interest in other people. We are to be ready to be with them in their joys and willing to share their griefs. We are to be ready to do so not merely with our friends, where such sharing is normally reciprocal, but with those whom we would not see as our friends and have nothing to offer us in return. The unloved are often the unlovely. If they are also lonely and isolated that will be joyless indeed. It is at a cost that we actually give ourselves to "the Ancient Mariner" — the man who demands our attention and insists that we listen. Our joy in doing this may require of us the virtue of accepting the principle of "delayed action". Insensitive indeed is the person who cannot respond to another human's need to talk and to share, and cannot find some satisfaction and ultimate joy in doing so.

Listening, being generous with our interest, is an end as well as a duty. I have sometimes been asked if there is not something dishonest in pretending an interest where we have none. The answer must surely be that what matters is not our feelings but our wills. I may at the level of my feelings pretend to an interest that I do not actually experience. But the reason for the pretence is that I do genuinely want to be interested. Having the will and the means to do some good are what matter. Sometimes our feelings catch up and sometimes they do not. The virtue is greater in the latter case than in the former.

I remember attending a Retreat led by Archbishop Michael Ramsey. He asked if we wanted to serve God. If we could not be sure, the next question was, "Do you wish you wanted to serve God?" And if there was still a doubt, "Do you wish that you wished that you wanted to serve God?" Generosity is very difficult to measure. We all know about the widow's mite — and sometimes cite the story in defence of our own meanness! But there are tests that we can apply. In the area of our interest, we can ask ourselves how often any of our neighbours turn to us because they know we will be ready to listen, ready to share, ready to make them feel we care. If this does not happen, we may have discovered something very important about ourselves. If we set ourselves to acquire the virtue we lack, it will enhance our own joy, not diminish it! Generosity is a divine economy — more blessed we are indeed, in the giving than in the receiving.

(d) Of our Praise

A great deal has been written about the virtue of humility, but the word has not always been well defined. Pride is seen as a deadly sin — but it is also a great virtue! From an early age we are encouraged to take pride in our work, in our appearance, in belonging to a particular school or club. Sins are usually the perversion of virtues — perhaps always so. So humility has come to mean a kind of abjectness, a self-denigration, a desire to under-estimate oneself in such a way that eventually confidence is undermined and a hesitant timidity takes over. It is not possible to find joy in such a situation. People need to be affirmed in order to be themselves. To give praise often produces a truer humility than does criticism and denigration. It makes for another's wholeness, and brings joy to another's heart.

In our relationship with God praise and worship are closely related, perhaps are synonymous. Christians believe — and they are not alone in doing so — that the worship of God is their ultimate destiny. We do not worship God for any good that may come of doing so, for worship is not a means to an end, but an end in itself — *the* end. That it why it seems to me as I said earlier, to be wholly mistaken, when in the counselling situation, religion is often given a very "low profile". The subject is introduced only at the behest of the client. What lies behind this is the idea that bringing God into the conversation is not always helpful. Of course it is not always helpful in the furtherance or achievement of some lesser though perhaps more evident and more pressing need. But that is not the point. A Christian cannot at the same time believe that man (human kind) is made for God, that the vision of God is his/her ultimate good — and decline to help a fellow human being to know this and to seek it. Religion may or may not at a given moment help the immediate and presenting need. But a refusal to introduce the subject unless the client raises it himself would be, as I have already noted, like a doctor refusing to prescribe unless the patient suggested it, on the grounds that the doctor must not thrust his own ideas on to his patient!.

It is true that there are many and great gains to those who worship God, but they are by-products of worship, not its main aim. Is it ever right to seek the by-products and to worship God in their pursuit? Intercessory and petitionary prayer are requests made to God for good things to happen both to us and to other people. It is right that we should make such prayers because in our worship we should disclose as openly as possible all that we are, which includes all that we want.

A wealthy business friend of mine told me he no longer prayed that his business should prosper because it had done so already beyond his expectation. I asked him, "Do you want it to prosper still more?" "Of course", he said. "Then you should pray that it will. Only so can you be real in your prayers — and open to God's response whatever it may be."

We do of course worship God because we need to! Paradox

90

is as evident here as in so much of our religion. God does not *need* our worship, although in a sense the very act of Creation is an expression of God's need, to love us, and all things, into being. We do need to worship in order to be truly human. Praising God for who He is and for what He has done is a natural not a super-natural activity. It is required of us all, and our lives are enhanced by doing it as surely as they are diminished when we do not.

Worship means ''expressing the worth of''. God is alone the object of all our total worship. But is Mary, the Mother of God, to be worshipped? And are the saints to be worshipped? Assuredly so, if we mean that they should all be given their worth, and that worth expressed in whatever ways we know. That is why, in everyday parlance, magistrates are addressed as ''Your worship''. Giving people their worth, affirming them, praising them — doing these things will not inflate their egos, lead them into the sin of pride, enhance their vanity — just the reverse! But our first concern is not the effect upon them of praising people, but upon the discharge of a duty, which should also be our joy. Giving worship is paying a due either to God or to a fellow human being.

Fear for another's humility may be one reason for not offering him or her our praise. It is not the only one. That ancient doctrine of the church, sometimes called 'the fall', sometimes 'original sin', tells us that human nature is corrupt, that the image of God, and His likeness, in which we were all created has become a distorted image. Where we should worship God and affirm our fellow creatures naturally, we do not. We can only do so by God's grace. We can only do so when our past failures are repented of and forgiven. In the context of praise it is perhaps most often the case that the sins of ''envy, hatred and malice'' (Book of Common Prayer, The Litany) stand in our way.

We may find ourselves hating God. We may feel more anger against Him than a desire to praise Him. If this is how we feel in any given situation, we offer even our anger to God, knowing that He is not only a loving but also an understanding Father. Our anger is based on our ignorance and we ask him "to turn our wounds into worship".

Have you ever said: "I am going to tell N or M exactly what I think of them"? The words are often uttered and always in a pejorative sense. We want to avenge a hurt; we are angry and mean to show it. Why is it that the words are seldom if ever used in the sense of, "I am going to tell N or M how well he/she has done and how full of admiration I am for him or her". Why? Because, so often, we are jealous. We envy another's success and cannot bring ourselves to utter words of appreciation. We even feel that we shall be hurting ourselves if we do so. Magnifying them means minimising ourselves. We do not like to hear someone else uttering the praises of those whom we dislike or despise. We want to hear evil of them! Yet praising another person is a heart-enlarging experience for us. We do not lose but immediately gain. How can we envy, how hate the person to whom we show praise rather than malice? Again we perceive the "divine economy". We give — and it is given to us.

(e) Of our Penitence and Forgiveness

Some people find it easier to apologise than to forgive. For others it is the other way round. I have often heard people say, "I will forgive him, of course; all he has to do is to apologise". We do not need to be reminded that penitence and forgiveness are at the centre of the Gospel. The passion and death of our Lord are mysteries beyond our comprehension but we all know that they are about God's reconciling love, His reconciling of sinful man back into a loving relationship. We would probably all say that the Parable of the Prodigal Son is our favourite parable, because it speaks to our need to come home to the Father and find in Him welcome, pardon and love.

St Paul wrote that "while we were yet sinners, Christ died for us". This is the answer to those who await the apologies of others. If our Lord had awaited human kind's apology, he would be waiting still. In the matter of our forgiveness, it was the righteous God who made the move. It is so still. We come to God in penitence drawn by His prevenient pardon. In our dealing with other people we must seek to follow His example. If God in His goodness takes the first step in reconciling us to Himself, what possible reason could we have for not taking the initiative in seeking reconciliation with those with whom we find ourselves at variance? It is almost as if we have the advantage over God in that we can begin the conversation with the words: "I know that I am at fault".

If we really take our Lord's own words to heart, we would accept that our own forgiveness depends upon our willingness to forgive others. Our plea for pardon is in the prayer He taught us, coupled with our protestation that we forgive others. Can we forfeit God's forgiveness? I think not — His love is too great to be thwarted and frustrated by any man's sin. Could a loving God ever destroy a soul that He had made? I came upon these verses recently, and they deserve attention. They made a considerable impression upon me.

> On a rusty iron throne
> Past the furthest star of space
> I saw Satan sit alone
> Old and haggard was his face
> For his work was done, and he
> Rested in Eternity.
>
> And to him from out the sun
> Came his father and his friend
> Saying, now the work is done
> Enmity is at an end
> And he guided Satan to
> Paradises that he knew.

Gabriel without a frown
Uriel without a spear
Raphael came winging down
Welcoming their ancient peer
And they seated him beside
One who had been crucified.

The danger of believing that the worst of sinners must ultimately be won to penitence and pardon is that it denies our free will — we would thus not be free to say, "No" to God. But if we believe that His service is alone, perfect freedom, then there is a contradiction in believing that we are ultimately free to refuse God, simply because such freedom would be slavery. The compulsion of love is not force as we generally understand it. It is the most gentle of magnets that draws us most willingly. We respond, not by losing anything but by gaining everything. And joy is at the heart of it. The unforgiving nature is the most joyless of natures. The inpenitent sinner experiences at best a travesty of the joy that God offers in return for a change of heart. However much others suffer because I can either not repent or not forgive is nothing compared with my loss, in which ever way I fail.

One of the loveliest of Old Testament stories is found in 1 Kings. It is the story of Elijah and the widow woman. He first asks her for a drink. Then he asks for something to eat. She replies that the barrel of meal contains enough for one more meal for herself and for her son. Then they must die. "Make me thereof a little cake first" says Elijah — and promises that the barrel of meal and the cruse of oil will not fail, until the Lord sends rain again. She obeys — and the miracle is wrought. But it is her obedience that is most miraculous, most to be wondered at. To give at that point is generosity indeed.

And in the New Testament? When we speak of the incarnation of our Lord we usually consider his humility. But we could equally well comment on his generosity. The Incarnation is the greatest act of generosity the world has ever known. Our Lord gave up the very riches of heaven — and counted them not a prize to be snatched at (Phil. 2.4-8) in order to become man and dwell among us — in the humblest and poorest of circumstance.

I have instanced certain areas in which our generosity is called for in response to which we find a renewal of our joy. No doubt there are many others which the reader will think of for him or her self. If it is true that "God loves a cheerful giver", it is also true that we experience that love when we give cheerfully and joyfully, not counting the cost.

Let me conclude these chapters with a small personal reminiscence. During the last war when I was training for a commission, I spent a week in the Lake District at a so-called "Battle Camp". We were to experience some of the less comfortable circumstances that we might find in a real battle. We began each day wading through a river, up to our necks, holding our rifles over our heads! The camp had a motto which I shall never forget:

A conscious man can always run.

It is when you know that you are totally spent and all strength is exhausted, when you know that you cannot take another step — but when you do, you find that you can! There is always more in us than we think. We are not giving to the maximum, and probably that will not be expected or required of us. But we could manage a little more.

CHAPTER 6

THE JOY OF REMEMBERING

"God gave us memories that we might have roses in December."

The gift of memory is surely among the greatest of the attributes we cherish. It can also be a curse. In the ministry of healing and, of course, in the whole realm of psychotherapy, we find that people are sick because of their painful memories. They long to be able to forget or at least to find some degree of relief from the sorrow that remembering engenders. We should like to be able to select from among the things we recall those things that make for happiness, and be able to forget the others. To some degree perhaps we do. If nature tends towards healing, we may find that we can decide what we will remember and what we can forget. But the memories from which we most want to be free, are the most difficult to deal with. Even if we can banish them from our conscious minds, they often emerge afresh, in dreams and nightmares.

The ageing process includes a loss of memory especially of the more recent occurrences. Two things, it has been said, seem to occur to most of us as we get older. The first is the inability to recall. The second — I can't remember what the second is.

An elderly lady had vivid memories of the place she was born. "I haven't been back for years, but I remember it as if it were yesterday." A visit was organised and a lovely "trip down memory lane" was arranged. Asked a day later about the place of her birth her reply was still, "I remember it as if it were yesterday". But she had forgotten that she had been there yesterday!

I used to minister to a nonagenerian when I was Vicar of St Andrew's, Bedford. She lived alone. When Christmas came she was inundated with invitations to spend the day with one of her numerous family and friends. She refused them all simply because she knew no greater joy than to spend the day quietly remembering the Christmas Days of the past. But she always received Communion, in her little flat, on Christmas morning.

To take the sacrament to people who can no longer come to church, in their own homes, is one of the greatest of privileges. And it is, of course, essentially an act of remembrance. Direct commands or instructions to his followers were not normally our Lord's way but two things he did bid them. "Love one another" was one. "Do this in remembrance of me" was the other.

If the passion, death and resurrection of our Lord are the focus of the incarnate life, so the Eucharist is the focus of the life of the Church and of every Christian soul. The Last Supper was a symbolic acting out, on the night before Good Friday, of the events of that momentous day. He took bread, the sacrament of his body, and he took wine, the sacrament of his blood. He blessed them, he broke the bread, and he shared them with his followers. Ever since, his disciples have shared the event symbolically and sacramentally, with him, doing these things by which to remember him. As Dom Gregory Dix wrote in *The Shape of the Liturgy* (A and C Black, 1945):

> Was ever another command so obeyed? For century after century, spreading slowly to every continent and country and among every race on earth, this action has been done in every conceivable human circumstance, for every conceivable human need, from infancy and before it to extreme old age and after it, from the pinnacles of earthly greatness to the refuge of fugitives in the caves and dens of the earth. Men have found no better thing than this to do for Kings at their crowning and for criminals going to the scaffold; for armies in triumph or for a bride and bridegroom in a little country church; for the proclamation of a dogma or for a good crop of

wheat; for the wisdom of the parliament of a mighty nation or for a sick old woman afraid to die, for a schoolboy sitting an examination or for Columbus setting out to discover America; for the famine of whole provinces or for the soul of a dead lover; in thankfulness because my father did not die of pneumonia, for a village headman much tempted to return to fetish because the yams had failed; because the Turk was at the gates of Vienna; for the repentance of Margaret; for the settlement of a strike; for a son for a barren woman; for Captain so and so, wounded and prisoner of war; while the lions roared in the nearby amphitheatre; on the beach at Dunkirk; while the hiss of scythes on the thick June grass came faintly through the windows of the church; tremulously by an old monk on the fiftieth anniversary of his vows, furtively, by an exiled bishop who had hewn timber all day in a prison camp near Murmansk; gorgeously, for the canonization of St Joan of Arc — one could fill many pages with the reasons why men have done this, and not tell a hundredth part of them. And best of all, week by week and month by month, on a hundred thousand successive Sundays, faithfully, unfailingly, across all the parishes of Christendom, the pastors have done this just to *make* the *plebs sancta Dei* — the holy common people of God.

When we go to the Eucharist, we take our sick and sinful selves to the source of our healing. Individually and together we confess our needs, for pardon and peace. The Eucharist is the great healing sacrament, for there we find, as we remember Christ's healing, saving words, that we are healed and saved. To say this is not to denigrate the importance of medicine, surgery or psychiatry. They have their very important place. That place may literally and figuratively seem far removed from the church and the altar; so far removed, it seems to many, as to have no connection and no relationship. The Christian thinks otherwise. He sees God's created universe as a whole. He sees that his wholeness — her wholeness — is very closely related to God the Creator, the Saviour and the Sanctifier. In remembering his Lord he finds his Lord, and with him finds the gifts of healing and forgiveness. Of course the altar is not the only place where God is to be found. But it is the pledged and covenanted place where He is most assuredly present.

So the focus of the Christian life is an act of remembering or an enacted remembrance — and it teaches the Christian the spirit in which he is to do all his remembering.

Consider Remembrance Sunday. We have been concerned to make the point that *every* Sunday is Remembrance Day. But once a year on the Sunday nearest to November 11th, the day when the Armistice was signed that brought the First World War to an end, there is another call to remembrance. We are bidden to remember those who died, as it is often put, for king and country, in the two World Wars and in the many conflicts that have taken the lives of men and women, between the wars and since the wars. With them we remember the wounded and the bereaved.

Mrs Coltman was the Church Warden at St Barnabas' church in Coventry, the daughter church in the parish of which I was Vicar. She was engaged when the first war began and her fiancé was called up. He got weekend leave sometime later, and they were married on the Saturday. The next day he rejoined his unit. She never saw him again.

Many other women lived and died unmarried, simply because there were not enough men to go round. They never mourned their husbands. They never even met them. No doubt like Jepthah's daughter (Judges 11.37), they "bewailed their virginity".

Once a year then, there is in the secular world an annual Act of Remembrance. Wreaths are laid at the Cenotaph and at War Memorials in towns and villages. Often there is some link with the church. The British Legion parades and lays wreaths at its altar. There it presents its Standards. "Folk religion" people say. Perhaps — but why not? Is not that better than no religion? Of course it is. It is also an opportunity of addressing the subject of *how* we should do our remembering. That matters very much indeed. How and how not!

To remember on one day in the year would for some be the supreme luxury — because they cannot possibly forget. When I was curate of Roehampton in the 1950's, I was chaplain of the Roehampton Hospital, then under the direction of the Ministry of Pensions. It specialized in the casualties of war, especially the limbless. One day I visited in just one ward ex-servicemen from the Boer War, both the two World Wars and from Korea — all had lost at least one limb. Did they need to remember? How could they forget? When I first went to the hospital I felt daunted by the prospect of visiting so many of the sick and maimed. I was an ex-service man myself and served in World War Two for five years. But I came out suffering only the loss of hearing in one ear. How could I talk to those a thousand times more disadvantaged? Yet that hospital was the happiest place in the parish. The camaraderie, the buoyancy of spirit, the wonderful perception of what matters in life and what does not — these things made every visit a tonic and ministry to such people, an enormous privilege.

So some people know *how* to remember, but not all. For some, to remember is to rekindle hatred, resentment and a spirit of revenge. When this is the consequence of remembering it were better to forget. Yet probably it is only when we work through our remembering that we come not to forgetting but to forgiving. Christian counselling with prayer and the Laying on of Hands, at best in the context of the Eucharist, points to the one who though sinless died a murderer's death, and prayed for his murderers. When our Lord becomes the focus of our remembering we are giving him the opportunity of turning our hatred into forgiveness, our vengeance into love, and our misery into joy.

Remembrance can then have an effect upon the way we deal with the memories of wrongs done to us. All of us have them. All of us probably feature as the wrong-doer in the memory of someone else. When we remember so that we engender forgiveness in ourselves and seek it for others, we are contributing to the joy of the world. When we become more aware of our own shortcomings, the degree of our own responsibilities for the evils that surround us, the remembering is doing its healing work and the Kingdom of Heaven breaks in.

CHAPTER 7

IN CONCLUSION

"Who shall find joy's language? There is neither speech nor word".
So wrote Robert Bridges and with his words I began this book.
I began then, by recognising the impossibility of the task and
then set out to say at least something, to write a few words.
I have not tried to be objective. I have sought to share with
you, my readers, something of the joy which the practice of
the Christian faith has given me in the course of a life-time
already in excess of the allotted span!

I freely acknowledge my indebtedness to many people, only
a few of whom have I been able to mention. It was kind and
generous of the Provost of Coventry, the Very Reverend John
Petty, to write the Preface. One of the joys of my retirement
to the Diocese of Coventry has been, and is, the pleasure of
working with him in the furtherance of the Healing Ministry
in the Diocese.

Denis Duncan has written the Foreword. In publishing my
writings he has shown great faith! I appear in print only
because of his kindness and encouragement. Typing from my
manuscript is an unimaginable labour and I have again to
thank Pam Grant for doing this.

The cover picture is from the West Front of Rheims
Cathedral and is known as ''Le Sourire de Rheims''. Angels
are rarely portrayed with a smile. But why? Must they not
be among the happiest of God's creatures?